My Hair-Raising and Heartwarming Adventures as a Pet Sitter

CHRISTI GRACE

HARVEST HOUSE PUBLISHERS
EUGENE, OREGON

Cover design by Emily Weigel Design

Cover photo © Nataliya Hora / Shutterstock

Interior design by Rockwell Davis

While all of the stories are true, some of the names and identifying details have been changed to protect the privacy of individuals.

My Hair-Raising and Heartwarming Adventures as a Pet Sitter
Copyright © 2020 by Christi Grace
Published by Harvest House Publishers
Eugene, Oregon 97408
www.harvesthousepublishers.com

ISBN 978-0-7369-7896-5 (pbk)
ISBN 978-0-7369-7897-2 (eBook)

Library of Congress Cataloging-in-Publication Data

Names: Grace, Christi, author.
Title: My hair-raising and heartwarming adventures as a pet sitter /
    Christi Grace.
Description: Eugene, Oregon : Harvest House Publishers, [2020]
Identifiers: LCCN 2019028474 (print) | LCCN 2019028475 (ebook) | ISBN
    9780736978965 (pbk) | ISBN 9780736978972 (ebook)
Subjects: LCSH: Pet sitting--Biography.
Classification: LCC SF414.34 .G73 2020 (print) | LCC SF414.34 (ebook) |
    DDC 636.088/7--dc23
LC record available at https://lccn.loc.gov/2019028474
LC ebook record available at https://lccn.loc.gov/2019028475

Printed in the United States of America
19 20 21 22 23 24 25 26 27 / VP-RD / 10 9 8 7 6 5 4 3 2 1

To John and Vic, my newly found treasures

ACKNOWLEDGMENTS

To the Mate of my soul, Jesus my Lord. You are the Great I Am. In and through You, all things are possible. Thank You, thank You, thank You, thank You.

To my family. Thank you for the role you played in this journey. I could not have pulled it off without your support.

To every pet I've been blessed to care for. Thank you for the lessons of love you taught me. Without you, I would have no story to tell.

To the amazing humans who trusted me to care for their furry and feathered "kids." You will always have a special place in my heart. Thank you for allowing me the wonderful blessing of having your pets in my life.

To my prayer partners. Prayer changes everything. Thank you, Melissa.

To Kim Moore. A kindred sister with the sweetest heart for God's animal creation. You are truly the *very best*!

To Jean Bloom. Thank you for your unique and seasoned insight.

To Todd Hafer. Thank you for getting me through the deer-in-the-headlights beginning! I couldn't have navigated it without you.

To Harvest House Publishers. Thank you for giving me the opportunity to share these stories. I'm truly humbled and thankful to be part of such a professional and sincere *family*.

CONTENTS

Preface 7

Christi's Furry Family 9

1. The Gift of Gideon 13

2. A Goat's Worth 23

3. Running from Rocko 35

4. The Lost and Found 47

5. Shiloh's Promise 65

6. Pajamas at Work 87

7. Molly's Epiphany 95

8. The Heart of Hollis .105

9. Forgiving ToTo 123

10. The Invisible Pet 135

11. The Joy of Joy 147

12. Saying Goodbye 173

PREFACE

Ask the animals, and they will teach you, or the birds
in the sky, and they will tell you; or speak to the
earth, and it will teach you, or let the fish in the sea
inform you. Which of these does not know that the
hand of the Lord has done this? In his hand is the
life of every creature and the breath of all mankind.

Job 12:7-10 niv

When I left the crazy and stressful corporate world, I never imagined the path God had prepared for me. But I've always loved animals—they've been part of my life for as long as I can remember—and starting my own pet-sitting business was a dream come true. I call it *the best job ever.*

I'm so excited to share my journey with you. Each pet-sitting story is not only true but filled with life lessons God taught me through the animals I cared for over a 12-year period. Some of the stories are humorous, some are difficult, and some are miraculous. Each encounter changed my life in an amazing way and proved to me that God and His love will go to the ends of the earth for *all* of His creation.

I hope that after reading this book, you, too, will be changed, at least in some small way.

CHRISTI'S FURRY FAMILY

The Red Horse Barn…

Sugar—Sugar is a sorrel mare, and she is my barn princess. I raised her from birth, and she is every bit a diva, but she also has the biggest, sweetest heart. Sugar thinks the world revolves around her, and as far as I'm concerned…it does! When she was three months old, she became gravely ill. I thought I was going to lose her. But through tears and constant prayer she pulled through and has been with me for 14 years. She is playful and mischievous—and a real *pain*, according to her brother, Milo.

Milo—Milo is a 19-year-old sorrel gelding. He is the great protector of his herd—unless a biting horsefly lands on him, in which case he runs to his human mama for help. Milo came to me when he was four years old. He hadn't been treated well in his early years, and it took a lot of patience and love to bring him around. But now he is a strong and confident boy. His sister, Sugar, drives him crazy with her head always in *his* hay pile. As much as he tries to put on the macho show, I know he adores her and wouldn't have it any other way.

Penny—Penny, a beautiful light sorrel mare with a flaxen mane and tail, is 26 years young and was my trusted riding partner for almost 14 years. She is now enjoying her retirement. I have such a strong bond with this girl. It's as though we can read each other's minds. She loves to have her belly scratched and will chase me around the pasture and block my way with her entire body until I rub her tummy. If I give up too soon, she gives me a nudge with her nose to remind me I'm not finished yet! She can be cranky with the other two horses in her herd, and at times she takes the "boss mare" role to another level.

Three Poms and a Non-Pom...

Ruby—Ruby is a sweet 17-year-old Pomeranian. She is the matriarch of my canine crew. She came to me as a puppy mill rescue when she was just nine weeks old. Despite major health problems at this age, she still runs circles around the younger dogs. Ruby's favorite food is oatmeal (and anything else I'm eating). She loves to curl up on my bed under the electric blanket. She also loves to stir up the other dogs and get them into trouble so she can have the prime spot on the bed.

Webber—I could provide a lot of descriptions for Webber. He is a 7-pound Pomeranian with the biggest Napoleon complex you could ever imagine. Webber doesn't like to be woken up before he's ready to get up, and he lets you know it with the best Tasmanian devil impression he can muster. I am always telling Webber it's a REALLY GOOD THING he's so cute! Webber is now ten years old. He was a gift after I lost Rocky, the best dog in the world. In spite of his sometimes less-than-stellar personality, I love him with all my heart.

Holly—Holly is my sweet little five-pound ball of fur. Holly is also a Pomeranian. She was six months old when I got her just over ten years ago. She was the pet of an acquaintance, and I ended up falling in love with her. Next thing I knew, she was coming home with me to keep Webber company. They have been inseparable ever since. Holly suffers from seizures, and at times it's a challenge having a special-needs dog. But like every one of my furry blessings from God, my life wouldn't be complete without her.

Bella—Bella is my loyal Australian shepherd. She is now 14 years young, and I love her with all my heart. She never leaves my side. I knew she was going to be a loyal companion when I first got her at eight weeks old. I had her in my arms when I slipped and fell. Although I wasn't hurt (and neither was she), she stayed by my side until I got up and she made sure I was okay. Bella was also a puppy mill rescue. Her greatest wish is that she didn't live with three high-strung, constantly barking Pomeranians. I affectionately call Bella my "Non-Pom."

1

THE GIFT
OF GIDEON

Take my yoke upon you. Let me teach you,
because I am humble and gentle at heart, and
you will find rest for your souls. For my yoke is
easy to bear, and the burden I give you is light.

MATTHEW 11:29-30 NLT

Every pet I cared for offered a new opportunity to fall in love, and Gideon was no exception.

Gideon was a dog, and his owners found me and my pet-sitting services through their horse veterinarian. Now I had the chance to get to know him and the other animals I would be caring for. As I drove up their crunchy gravel driveway, I saw big brown eyes peering through the slats of the metal farm gate chained across the entrance to their front yard. I knew that had to be Gideon.

He was a golden-colored Labrador mix with a happy-go-lucky look on his face—his mouth was open just enough to form a perfect smile. And his anticipation was evident as his whole body moved back and forth with each wag of his tail.

The owners hadn't told me whether to go inside the gate when I arrived, so I stopped my car and turned off the ignition before grabbing my notebook, pen, and business card. Then I got out and walked up to the gate.

I don't know if that was the moment I fell in love with Gideon or if it was a few seconds later when he hopped back a few steps as if to give me room to open the gate. That's when I noticed he held his front right leg up close to his body and moved on his three remaining legs with an exaggerated hobble.

A young couple arrived and welcomed me warmly as they let me inside. Right away, the husband, Kirk, explained that Gideon had been hit by a car about three years earlier, and they'd hoped his leg would heal without veterinary intervention. I tried to hide my puzzlement, but it must have been evident because Kirk went on to say they felt sure Gideon could put down his leg and walk on it; he was just too scared. Meanwhile, Kirk said, Gideon managed to get around just fine.

Seeing Gideon hobble tugged at my heart, but he didn't seem too bothered even though he had to rest after several minutes of following us around. He seemed to enjoy tagging along as the couple introduced me to the two horses I would be caring for as well.

After I'd received all the routine instructions I needed and made notes, I scheduled my return in two weeks to care for Gideon and his horse siblings. Gideon, ever the gentleman, escorted me back to the gate. As I opened it just enough to squeeze through, he watched me with those big brown eyes as if he were thinking, *Where are you going? You just got here!*

Gideon remained at the gate as I backed away in my car, and I can still picture his sweet send-off.

The day I returned, I was greeted in what I soon learned was typical Gideon fashion—his big eyes peering through the gate slats as I pulled up the gravel driveway. I was so excited. I couldn't wait to give him a hug and spend time with him.

As I gathered hay for the horses and mixed their feed, Gideon followed me. It was a hot July day, and I could see that he was laboring to move on his three good legs. When he panted more and more, I looked for his water dish, but I had failed to note its location on my last visit. Once I found it, though, I realized it was positioned perfectly under the house roof's downspout. I looked at Gideon, who was now lying in the cool mud nearby, and wondered if this was his usual water supply. Later, I learned it was.

On that first day, I took time to assess Gideon's bad leg, wondering if he *could* put it down. He wasn't bothered by my touching his leg or gently pulling it to see if it would stretch out, so I thought maybe I could help him start to walk on it. But then I realized the leg was fused close to his body so he couldn't lower it.

It was also clear that this precious dog accepted his condition and didn't feel sorry for himself. Aside from being tired after lengthy periods of hobbling around, Gideon seemed to consider himself at no disadvantage.

Over the next year, I cared for Gideon many times. I loved caring for him. I loved his gentle demeanor and how he took life one hobble at a time. I noted that he was fine with drinking rainwater from the gutter, but he *loved* it when I gave him water from the hose instead.

This three-legged dog had stolen my heart. I had my own opinions about his situation, and I was determined to give him as much love as I could while he was on my watch. It was an opportunity I welcomed, and I knew he'd entered my life for a bigger reason than to just give him food and water.

On several occasions Gideon wasn't himself. Instead of hobbling out to greet me, he stayed under the porch, unwilling to come out no matter how much I coaxed him. I mentioned this to Kirk and his wife, but they said that was normal behavior for him at times. They attributed it to either the heat or to his experiencing separation anxiety because they were away.

One day, unexpectedly, they called to say they were moving out of state and couldn't take Gideon. Could I find a home for him—in three days? Otherwise, he would have to go to a shelter. My heart sank. How would I find a three-legged dog a home in three days? I asked God to help me find the kind of home this precious dog deserved and went to work.

Two days went by with none of my efforts paying off, but I kept hearing these words: *Don't give up.* So I continued to plead Gideon's case to friends, family, and my other customers. I also had a network of pet rescuers I called on from time to time, but no one could help Gideon. Day three arrived, and my heart was so heavy. How could I let Gideon be handed off to a shelter?

So I did what my husband later told me he knew was coming all along. I brought Gideon home with me! I knew his stay had to be temporary; I already had a houseful of dogs and cats and a barn full of horses, and I couldn't fit more hungry mouths on our small farm. But this decision would give me time to find Gideon a wonderful, permanent home.

In the meantime, having Gideon with us was a beautiful gift. His gentle personality filled our farm with warmth. He loved lying in our barn near the horses and bobbing through the pastures. My dogs loved him too. We would all sit in the yard while Gideon lay down and let the other dogs jump on him and tug at his ears. He was such a good sport, and he loved the attention. None of the other dogs seemed to notice Gideon's burdensome appendage.

I continued to ask God not just for a home for him but also for the love he deserved. Gideon had taught me so much about rising above the unfairness of the world and taking it all in stride—even if it was an uneven stride.

I knew God would come through.

Gideon spent about six weeks with us. Then one of my customers who had said no to adopting Gideon told me her daughter wanted to give him a home. What's more, her daughter wanted to have his leg corrected.

God is so good!

It was a bittersweet Saturday when my customer and her daughter came to take Gideon to his forever home. My heart was overjoyed for him but heavy for me. Gideon had become a part of our lives. On some days, seeing his gentle, furry face made my heart forget all the reasons I needed to find him a home. But I also knew it was best for him to go where he would be the center of attention. He had never had that.

Seeing Gideon hobble around each day gave me a kind of comfort from deep within. It reminded me that, as imperfect as I am, an amazing God loves me. He looks down on me, sees me hobbling around, yet has compassion for me. He extends amazing grace. And He knows there will be a better home for me someday, a home where my imperfections will be shed like a useless appendage.

It's funny, but I believe Gideon knew where he was going that day—*home*. He immediately took to my customer's daughter; as we walked around, Gideon never left her side. She fell in love with him, too, as I knew she would. When it came time for them to leave, Gideon jumped right into their car. I felt a little prick in my heart when Gideon didn't even look back at me, but I knew he was going where he needed to be.

Over the next few days, I was simultaneously elated, relieved, and thankful. God had answered my prayer, and I think He answered Gideon's as well. His new owner kept in contact with me, sending me pictures of him curled up on her bed and of his new food bowl, his new toys, his new favorite blanket, and his new family, which included a horse, a cat, and a fellow canine. My heart could barely hold the fullness I felt.

The next step was for her to have that leg evaluated. Based on her vet's assessment, which confirmed my suspicions, she decided to have the vet amputate his leg. It had fused into position, and his condition couldn't be corrected. They scheduled the surgery, and we all waited with hopeful expectation for the big day.

When that day finally came, I learned that the surgery had gone well, with no complications. The veterinarian said once Gideon's wound healed, he would get around even better than before because he wouldn't be carrying the weight of that cumbersome and useless appendage. I was so thankful and happy for him.

Over the next few weeks, I received constant updates on his progress, and they were all good. Gideon was adjusting to the absence of his front leg and didn't seem bothered at all. He was enjoying the fully pampered life with a new home, a new owner, and a new start without his old baggage.

Gideon's new start reminded me of my own. Before I allowed Jesus into my independent life, I was much like Gideon. I carried around useless baggage, refusing to let God carry my burdens, "hobbling" through life, doing it my way. But then a Savior gently showed me a different way. He picked me up and gave me a new life. He discarded the old baggage that was thwarting my freedom, and I became free indeed!

What a gift we have waiting for us, if only we will surrender our burden, just as Gideon was able to give up his.

> Take my yoke upon you. Let me teach you, because I
> am humble and gentle at heart, and you will find rest for

your souls. For my yoke is easy to bear, and the burden I give you is light (Matthew 11:29-30 NLT).

As Gideon's wound healed to a tiny, barely visible scar, his new owner noticed an old pattern. Gideon began to hide under the bed and not want to come out. He even refused to go outside, a place he had loved so much. She became concerned, and I suggested a visit to the vet. The news wasn't good. The veterinarian ran some tests and found that Gideon had leukemia. There'd been no indication of the disease in any of his routine bloodwork before, but this time it was conclusive.

I thought about the year I had spent caring for Gideon, and the several times he'd clearly not been himself sprang to mind. The memories hit me like a punch in the stomach because the vet said Gideon had probably been dealing with cycles of symptoms and remission for a while. Neither I nor Gideon's owner could believe the news. We didn't *want* to believe it. The prognosis that Gideon might still have a few good years ahead of him did little to console us.

The tears came. I had thought this was going to be Gideon's happy ending. I thought he was going to finally have the life he deserved, the one I wanted for him. But a couple of months crawled by, and Gideon's health declined rapidly. Six months after his adoption, I received a tearful phone call. It was the day none of us had wanted to arrive.

I think of Gideon often. As I recall the day I first met the most amazing three-legged dog, I can still see his happy-go-lucky face at the gate. I know God put him in my life for many reasons, and I'm thankful—not only for the blessing of loving him but because he had the best six months of his life with a family that loved him the way he deserved to be loved.

We are all thankful for the gift of Gideon.

Dear Lord, thank You for Your amazing gift of salvation and grace. Forgive me when I try to hold my burdens too tightly instead of letting them go and trusting You to carry them for me. Teach me that true freedom is in You alone. In Jesus's name, amen.

2

A GOAT'S WORTH

~~~~~~~~

God demonstrates His own love toward us, in that
while we were still sinners, Christ died for us.

ROMANS 5:8

It was a cool Sunday morning that spring, and I was excited as I drove up the long dirt driveway on some new customers' property. Their home was a small but immaculate ranch-style farmhouse, but what was hidden behind its gray exterior? The anticipation excited me.

I climbed out of my car, muck boots in hand, and tentatively walked to the side of the house and down a tree-lined path. Several guinea hens greeted me as they loudly announced my arrival to anyone within a five-mile radius. As I looked just ahead to a fenced-in area, eight inquisitive faces peered back at me as they lined up trying to see what was so interesting. In the background, near a simple lean-to barn, more chickens than I could count were busily pecking the ground.

I dropped my muck boots and kicked off my flip-flops. Yes, flip-flops. Even though the temperature was barely above 60 degrees, I was sporting my trusty favorite footwear. Having been born and raised in Florida, I found flip-flops to be a hard habit to kick even in cooler temperatures. I slid my feet into the muck boots lined with warm fleece and turned my attention to the eight peering faces. By now, these goats were interested in my every move.

I pulled out my cheat sheet from my sweatshirt pocket and

scanned the descriptions I'd recorded during my get-acquainted visit with one of the owners, Iris, a couple of weeks earlier. I wanted to identify each goat.

This was my first pet-sitting job involving goats and chickens. I'd encountered these critters in petting zoos as a young child, but that had been the extent of my experience. Plus, one incident with a goat had been anything but pleasant. I was a little nervous, but I believed I would get the hang of caring for these creatures quickly, and my excitement far outweighed my nerves.

As I took roll call, I not only took in each goat's size and coloring, but I called each one by name. Amazingly, they did know their names. One by one, they responded with twitching ears and steady gazes in my direction. Next to one of the descriptions was the name Ginger. My notes on her included the words *matriarch* and *not the smartest goat*. Iris had given me a detailed description of each goat's personality too.

Ginger was a small white doe with brown, floppy ears and a brown face. Two of the younger goats were her offspring, but she was still quite young herself. Iris hadn't realized the goat was pregnant when she purchased her. Ginger's two adorable kids were born a month later—a huge surprise.

I watched Ginger as she stood at the fence. One of the billy goats was playfully head-butting her, but Ginger seemed unfazed.

Iris had also told me Ginger often stumbled into various predicaments (thus my *not the smartest goat* notation). I laughed and didn't think much about it at the time. After all, I reasoned, how much trouble can a goat get into?

I returned my notes to my pocket as I walked toward the gate. All eight goats quickly ran forward, huddling together and pushing forward in anticipation. I knew they planned to escape if I gave them half a chance. Fortunately, I managed to squeeze in before any of them could.

But now my heart was pounding as I stood just inside the gate with all the goats surrounding me. No one had warned me about "goat gate-charging," which I later learned is typical behavior for these creatures. I imagined spending my entire Sunday trying to catch the escaped goats all around this customer's yard.

A couple of the billy goats gently nudged me with their horns. I tried to act calm, even though I'd had that one unpleasant experience as a child. Actually, I'd been traumatized. A head-butting goat at a "petting farm" chased me across a big field before I climbed onto a huge haystack in a barn. My uncle Steve had to run across the field and grab the goat before he got to me. I wondered if a similar scene would play out today. But I kept my cool and reminded myself that I was all grown up now. It wouldn't be good if the neighbors saw the pet sitter frantically running through the goat pen.

Thankfully, none of the billy goats decided to butt me, and I said a quick *Thank You, Lord* as I sighed with relief. But as I stepped out, they followed me closely, anticipating their breakfast.

The goats' food was in a big plastic container in a small barn. My notes told me the exact amount to feed them and where to put the food so they wouldn't get into a scuffle over it. I poured it in the various places and then cleaned out their water troughs.

Next I had to feed the chickens and clean their coop. I was amazed at how the chickens knew where the feed would be and at how eagerly they followed me around. I've heard people say chickens are dumb, but that isn't true. They may not be the smartest animals, but they definitely aren't dumb.

I'd never been around chickens and goats like this, and I was having a lot of fun. I also had the job of gathering eggs from the chicken's nest boxes, and Iris had told me I could help myself to the eggs. Some were still warm. A few of the hens remained sitting on the nests, though, so I had to reach under them to get the eggs. For the most part, they were nice about it, but a couple of them gave my cold hands a peck!

As I finished my chores, I felt incredibly blessed to be doing what I loved and having new experiences some people may never enjoy.

I reviewed my notes just to make sure I'd covered all my duties, and then I glanced toward the chicken coop and double-checked the water containers before I left and made sure to latch the gate behind me. I would be returning in the evening to check on everyone and put the chickens to bed in their coop.

As I took one last look around, I noticed Ginger coming out of the barn—and then stumbling and falling over. I was taken aback as I watched her try to get up again and again and fall down every time. I ran to her and picked her up, and then I placed her back on her feet. But when I released my grip, she collapsed again. I panicked. What was going on? I checked to see if a snake was around. I didn't see one, but that didn't mean Ginger hadn't been bitten.

I wondered if I was going to watch her die right there, and then I prayed, *Dear Lord, please help me. Give me wisdom. I don't know what to do!*

Ginger's owners were out of the country. They had given me their hotel phone number in case of an emergency, but they were several time zones away and warned me phone service there was unreliable. Still, I tried to call them on my cell phone, but I couldn't get through.

Ginger continued to struggle. Sometimes she stood and walked a couple of steps, but then she'd fall again. I couldn't imagine what had happened to her. In a few short minutes she'd gone from being completely normal to being seriously ill. I felt helpless, and I started to cry. I knew nothing about goats except what Iris had told me, which wasn't much. But I did know Ginger was accident prone.

I pulled out my cell phone again and dialed my horse veterinarian. I had to leave a message with his answering service since it was Sunday, but he returned my call right away. I told him what was going on, but he informed me he didn't work with goats. However, he did provide a number for a vet who might be able to help.

I got her answering service as well, but eventually she called me back. She would try to help, but she charged $250 just to make a house call. She went on to explain that the average price of a goat is about $35, so most people don't spend money on veterinary care for them. It's cheaper to simply buy a new one.

I was shocked. I had never thought about pets that way. I believed their worth shouldn't be calculated by how much you pay for them but by how much you love them.

I had no authority to authorize a large vet bill, so I just thanked the vet for her return call. Then I hung up, feeling completely defeated. Meanwhile, Ginger was still ailing, but since I could do nothing for her, I left. All the way home, I prayed for wisdom, for help, and for *whatever* was needed. When I got there I called the veterinary teaching school at our local state university, which was about 60 miles from where I lived.

Amazingly, someone answered! I pleaded Ginger's case to the gentle, kind voice of the head veterinarian, who just happened to be working on a Sunday.

God is good!

This vet repeated what I had heard before: Most people don't spend money on veterinary care for their goats, especially not for medical emergencies. I explained I was goat sitting for the first time for customers who were out of the country, and I couldn't just let the goat die without trying to help her.

He asked me about Ginger's symptoms. I explained that she kept falling over and that she had a dazed look on her face. His assessment: Ginger had what is sometimes called goat polio. Some goats become deficient in vitamin B1, and this affects their central nervous system. This condition is fatal if not treated promptly. He asked me if I had any vitamin B1 injections handy, but of course I didn't. Then he suggested calling a local veterinarian for assistance. But I'd already contacted the local vets, and they weren't coming without a promise of $250.

I sat down and had a good, helpless cry. I didn't even know if Ginger was still alive. But then I heard the whisper I'd heard so many times before: *Don't give up.*

"But, God," I said out loud through tears, "what can I do? No one will help me. No one seems to think a goat has much worth except You and me."

Then I had an idea. If Ginger needed vitamin B1, maybe it didn't have to come via a shot. I ran to the kitchen cabinet where I kept supplements. I knew I didn't have any straight B1, but I thought I had some B-Complex capsules somewhere.

I frantically moved containers around, and there in the back was a huge bottle of what I needed. It wasn't full, but quite a few capsules remained. I also had no idea how much B-Complex to give a goat, so I just grabbed a handful of the vitamins. Then I remembered the large oral syringe I used to give medicine to my horses.

I dissolved about ten capsules in water and drew the solution into my syringe before rushing out the door. I arrived at Ginger's place about ten minutes later and sprinted down the path to the goat pen. I was greeted by goats at the fence again, but Ginger was not among them. I looked toward the barn and saw her lying on the ground inside. Was I too late? My heart ached.

But she was still alive, and I picked up her weak, limp head and gently put the syringe into her mouth to squirt in the vitamin solution. She had just enough strength to shake her head in agitation. I was thankful to see that. I had no idea if I was giving her enough or way too much, but it was all I could do, and I wasn't giving up.

Like Ginger, I have amazing worth to God. He doesn't give up on me. When I was most unworthy, a sinner who felt no need for a Savior, He sent His only Son to die for me. He didn't wait for me to become more valuable or increase in worth—as if I could. Jesus died for me while I was still the worst of sinners, at my lowest of lows. Imagine, the Creator of the universe placing that kind of value on us all, giving His life as a ransom for our unworthiness and paying for our sins!

Praise God that He didn't give up on me. Praise God that He never thought there was no way to save me or that I was beyond saving. Praise God that He didn't see me as a nearly worthless $35 goat that could be easily replaced.

> God demonstrates His own love toward us, in that while we were still sinners, Christ died for us (Romans 5:8).

As Ginger lay on the ground, I wondered how vitamins from my kitchen cabinet could bring her back from this hopeless state. Then I stroked her head and told her I would be back soon. I had to care for more customers' animals, but I would return as soon as I could.

As I went about my job, I kept trying to reach Iris, and at last I did. I updated her on the situation, and I repeated what the various vets had told me. She was grateful for my efforts, but she told me she knew I had done everything I could, and that if Ginger died, I shouldn't feel bad. She asked if I could bury Ginger, because they didn't want her to lie out in the yard until they returned in eight days. I told her my husband would help me with the task if it became necessary. The thought of that broke my heart, though.

When I returned to check on Ginger a couple of hours later, my heart was still heavy; I feared I would find her dead. But I had mixed up more vitamin solution in the oral syringe just in case.

I looked around the barn, but she wasn't there. My heart sank. I sensed she'd gone off somewhere to die, and I looked into the distance where the other goats were grazing. But to my surprise, Ginger was in their midst. She was grazing!

I ran through the gate and called to her. Her head popped up, and all the goats ran toward me, including a staggering Ginger. Yes, she was wobbly, but she was managing to stay upright and keep up with her herd. I couldn't believe it, but she was definitely much improved.

How could this be? Could the cure have been that simple? I went to her, and then I held her mouth open and squirted the vitamin B solution I'd brought into her mouth. She shook her head, spilling some of the solution, but most of it went down.

Ginger still had that far-off, stargazer look on her face, but I felt such relief. While I knew she wasn't well yet, I held the hope that God had answered my prayer, that my first day with Ginger wasn't going to be my last. No matter what anyone else had said that day, Ginger was worth saving.

I made four or five visits a day to give Ginger more vitamin doses, and each day she showed more improvement. I noticed she still stargazed now and then, but she was walking almost normally and interacting well with the other goats. I contacted Iris with the good news.

Ginger continued to live up to the description first given me: a goat who seemed to find herself in predicaments! One evening, about two days before her owners were expected home, I did my last check and put the chickens in the coop for the night. Everyone was accounted for—except Ginger.

Panic gushed over me like a huge bucket of ice water. I looked around the large pen, but Ginger was nowhere to be found. As I ran around looking in every nook and cranny of the barn, I heard a faint cry. I stopped and focused, and then I heard another cry. It was definitely coming from a goat—most certainly Ginger.

I called her name, and her next cry was more urgent and louder. I walked in its direction, and in the faint light of dusk, I could barely see a white goat standing at the fence in the back corner of the pen. As I got closer, the cry got louder, and I realized what was going on. To my horror, Ginger was facing the fence with her head stuck through the wire!

I ran to her, not knowing what to expect. Was she being strangled? To my relief, she was safe though extremely annoyed. I stretched the pliable wire wide with my hand and pushed Ginger's head free. She stood still for a moment, and then she shook her head and took off toward the barn.

I was so thankful that my eventful week caring for Ginger was almost over. I never knew what I was going to find when I arrived to care for her. But Ginger had also become my favorite goat.

Home from her vacation, Iris still couldn't believe the goat was alive, that I'd been able to find a cure for her. Later, she researched Ginger's condition and found that she must have eaten moldy hay, which depleted the B vitamins in her system and caused the problem.

I continued to care for Ginger and her herd for several years after that scary week. Ginger also continued to get her head caught in the fence, and Iris eventually remedied that by tying a stick between her horns. But she remained the matriarch of her herd, and for the most part, she grew out of her misfortunate ways.

I'll never forget what God taught me through a $35 goat who turned out to be worth so much more.

Dear Lord, how can I ever thank You for what You did for me when You sent Your Son to give His perfect, priceless blood for my ransom? Thank You for teaching me that my worth to You transcends my own sense of unworthiness. While I was yet a sinner, Jesus still saw my value. Like Ginger, I stray at times, but thank You for never giving up on me. In Jesus's name, amen.

3

RUNNING FROM ROCKO

~~~~~~~~~~

He keeps his eye upon you as you come
and go and always guards you.

Psalm 121:8 tlb

I admit I might not have been all that forthcoming when Janet called requesting my services. Her first question was, "Do you have any experience with chickens and roosters?" I'd cared for chickens several times and loved it, but I'd never cared for roosters. My previous "fowl experience" had been limited to hens. So my quick "Yes!" wasn't 100 percent accurate. But in my defense, what was the big deal? After all, roosters are just male chickens.

Janet asked me to visit her farm so she could provide the details for caring for her animals during her seven-day vacation with her husband.

The day of our scheduled appointment, I drove down a long, tree-lined driveway to their small hobby farm. This was the dead of winter, and not a leaf could be found on any of those trees. It was cold, gray, and dreary—a typical January in Atlanta.

I pulled up to the driveway and gathered my notebook and pen before bracing myself for the cold that was about to hit me like an unwelcome wake-up call. I'm not a fan of winter—it's just too cold! I love warm sunshine and a gentle breeze. I love wearing flip-flops. And I detest wearing layers.

I grabbed my down-filled coat from the backseat and got out of the car—one arm in my coat, the other hand holding my notebook.

Then I switched the notebook to my other hand so I could finish donning my puffy coat against the chill. Janet, who was bundled up in her own arctic wear, came outside to greet me.

I've been blessed with amazing customers, and I can honestly say that each one of them, including Janet, has been kind and great to work with. She asked if I was ready to meet the chickens, and we traded small talk as we walked around to the back of her garage and down a muddy path to a large yard with paddock fencing.

I noted the many chickens running around inside. They had seen us coming and appeared to be agitated. Janet took me into the pen and showed me around the setup. She had names for every chicken, and she knew each one by sight. I thought about jotting down names and descriptions, but I quickly realized this would be futile because all the chickens looked virtually identical to me. I also didn't know why I would ever need to tell them apart.

Then a small, boisterous, and odd-looking chicken came running up to us. It was covered in pure white feathers and had what appeared to be a feather "hat" on top of its head. Janet noted the puzzled look on my face and said, "He's a Polish rooster. That's Rocko."

Rocko was staring at me through all the crazy, white feathers flopping down over his eyes. He cocked his head from side to side as if to get a better look, but I had no idea how he could even see. As he cautiously walked away, Janet gave me the lowdown.

"He's quite mean-spirited," she said, chuckling. "He has something of a Napoleon complex, but he's the only rooster in the chicken yard, so he feels he needs to be the protector. Just ignore him, and he'll back down and go about his business."

I decided to give Rocko the benefit of the doubt and shot him a sympathetic look.

As we left through the gate, though, I could still see Rocko out of the corner of my eye. He was running beside us as if to give me one final warning that he was in charge. I laughed and followed Janet back to my car. She was happy I'd agreed to care for her chickens, and she assured me I would be fine.

My first day there was two weeks later. It was cold and rainy, so I donned my black jacket with a hood to cover my head. But it was miserably wet, and the rain ran down my frozen fingers and dripped into my sleeves.

My spirit wasn't dampened by the weather, though. I was excited to see the chickens and gather some eggs. I love gathering eggs. Filling a basket with eggs chickens have just produced is a different experience from picking up a carton of eggs in a grocery store. To me, the grocery store experience is sterile, detached. Gathering eggs on a farm is the real deal.

I flipped up my jacket hood and pulled on my rain boots, and then I stepped out of my car and made my way to the back of the house. Janet had left a basket for collecting eggs by her back door. I picked it up on my way to the chicken yard, swinging it by the handle as I walked down the muddy path. Several chickens were out of the yard and greeting me. Janet had told me that was okay; they loved to roam and graze, and they'd fly back over the fence to roost in the barn when it grew dark.

Despite the weather, I didn't have a care in the world as I opened the paddock gate, egg basket in hand. I entered the pen with confidence, but before I could even survey the surroundings, something hit me in the head! I spun around, bewildered. Had something fallen from the sky or...Before I could complete my thought, I was struck again!

I spun around just in time to see Rocko running at me at full speed—wings out, feathers flapping, and the meanest expression I've ever seen on a chicken's face. I dropped the egg basket and, slipping and sliding in the mud, I ran as fast as I could toward the small roosting barn. About halfway there, Rocko struck me once more in the back of my head, and I was grateful for the protection of my hood.

Still, I screamed with each step toward the barn, where I hoped to escape my attacker. I ran inside and scrambled to the farthest corner. Where was Rocko? Was he still chasing me? Was he going to peck out my eyes? I was out of breath, almost hyperventilating. *Oh Lord, what is wrong with this crazy bird?*

I mustered enough courage to focus on the barn's entrance and wait for Rocko the wacko rooster to come in. Thankfully, he seemed to have lost interest in me. I let out a shaky sigh of relief and wondered what I should do. I was afraid to leave the safety of my corner in the barn, but I had work to do!

I gave myself a pep talk: *This is a bird, a two-pound chicken! What can this little rooster, who obviously has something to prove, do to you?*

The words made sense, but the thought of being anywhere near Rocko terrified me.

I swallowed hard and slowly crept out of the barn, exposing myself to the irrational creature. I quickly scanned the area, and there he was with the hens several yards away, pecking the ground as if his terrorizing of the pet sitter had never happened. *Maybe he just didn't recognize me from the other day, and now he'll be fine*, I thought. I cautiously walked over to where I had dropped the egg basket, all the while studying Rocko. He seemed to be looking at me out of the corner of his eye as though he was waiting for me to make a wrong move. Then he would let me have it!

The whole time I was there, I kept one eye on Rocko. If this was what all roosters were like, I never wanted to pet-sit for one again.

I managed to finish all the chores and even gather eggs without another confrontation with Rocko. I picked up the full basket and headed to the gate to leave, but every couple of steps I looked around to see where that floppy-headed nutjob rooster might be. He was nowhere to be seen, and I was certainly glad about that.

As I neared the gate, I sighed again with relief. But just as I was almost to the finish line—*smack!* Yep, a body-slamming feather bomb had hit me right in the middle of my back. No need to turn around; I knew who it was. With another scream, I ran the last couple of steps to the gate, my frozen, clumsy hands desperately trying to unlatch it as fast as I could without dropping any eggs.

Once outside the gate, I could see Rocko standing on the other side with a proud look on his face. He had done it. He had scared me away from his domain, defeated his enemy. He shot me a look as if to say, *And don't come back!* Then he strutted away.

As I drove away that morning, I tried to put what happened in perspective. After all, I was at the top of the food chain. Compared to Rocko, I had superior intelligence. So how could I be so scared of a tiny-brained chicken? What could he do to me, anyway? Yes, he rammed me, but his blows hadn't really hurt. And yes, he had claws that were supposedly razor sharp. But if I had wanted to, I could have probably snatched him in mid-air with one hand.

This realization made me chuckle, and my somewhat sound reasoning worked. I'd be ready for Rocko that evening when I returned to secure the chickens for the night. *No bully rooster is going to keep you from doing your job!* I told myself.

This evening visit would consist of closing up the roosting barn and making sure all the chickens were safe inside. Janet told me she'd lost several chickens to foxes and raccoons before she had a secure barn for them.

It's amazing how chickens learn a routine. Janet said hers wouldn't go into the barn even one minute before dark. Just as she said, darkness came, and only then did a mass of chickens go flocking to the barn. Inside, they went right to their favorite spots. With my newly found confidence, I scanned the yard for Rocko, ready to stand my ground if he challenged me. To my surprise, though, he completely ignored me and went into the barn with the rest of the chickens. With a thankful prayer, I closed the barn door and secured the latch.

With everyone safely in for the night, I left, relieved that Rocko had behaved himself.

Empty egg basket in hand, the next morning I arrived to let the chickens out for the day and take care of the morning chores. And I was also excited to see how many eggs I would get this time. The day before I'd retrieved 14.

There, front and center inside the gate, stood Rocko. His full attention was on me, but I took a deep breath and told myself not to be intimidated. As I opened the gate and stepped inside, Rocko flew at me, and this time I felt his feathers graze my cheek. I screamed and ran back out.

When I turned around, Rocko was again at the entrance, his eyes on me. He wasn't going to leave his post, and I felt so defeated.

This was getting old.

A small shed full of garden tools and miscellaneous items stood near the chicken yard, and my eyes fell on a big broom propped up against it. It had a wide head—perfect for swatting a bully rooster.

I grabbed it and pulled my jacket's hood over my head. Weapon in hand, I felt more equipped for battle. I walked back to the gate, opened it, and stepped inside with confidence. Rocko charged me, but he didn't strike. I took a few more steps toward the barn, holding the broom high. I was ready to strike *him* if necessary.

Rocko flew at me from behind. I screamed (again!) and ran for the roosting barn. But this time, I was slowed down. (Have you ever tried to run while holding a broom?)

When I got to the barn, I turned around and swung the broom

back and forth in front of the pursuing Rocko. He flew back a few feet, and he was not happy. I could see just part of one eye behind that crazy feather "hat," and that eye was focused on me. "Get out of here!" I yelled. He retreated, seeming to lose interest in bullying me. Eventually, he joined the other chickens.

I took refuge in prayer. *Lord, what can I do about this mean rooster? He's intent on making my job impossible! I need Your protection and intervention.* And then I thought about how I had entered into this job without telling my customer that I lacked experience with roosters, about how I hadn't been prepared for what I'd taken on.

⋯

He keeps his eye upon you as you come and go and always guards you (Psalm 121:8 TLB).

Too many times I've taken on something I wasn't prepared for because I hadn't first asked God for guidance. Without His blessing and leading, we can get ourselves into trouble; we can enter a battle-field without a weapon. Then we're vulnerable—open to attacks.

That's what the enemy of our souls does—he attacks. Like Rocko, he attacks us from any angle, and if we don't have God on our side, no weapon will protect us.

As I prayed, I also told the Lord I knew I was in this situation because I hadn't been totally forthcoming. I thought I could handle a rooster on my own, but even in a seemingly insignificant situation, I needed God. We all do.

⋯

Broom in hand, I walked to the roosting barn and opened the door to let the chickens out. I kept a close eye on Rocko, and he kept a close eye on me. He charged me several times that morning, and each time I waved my giant broom at him. That kept him at a distance while I did my chores.

The rest of the week was just as eventful. Each day, I entered the chicken yard with broom in hand, swinging it back and forth as I ran to the roosting barn. Thankfully, I never hit Rocko; I would have felt terrible if I had. But there was no other way to keep him from attacking me!

Janet and her husband returned from their week-long vacation, and I told her all about my time with Rocko. I also confessed that I had never cared for a rooster before. She laughed and said Rocko had chased her occasionally but nothing like how he chased me. She loved that I had stuck with it and found comfort in a broom.

The next week Janet called and told me Rocko had been attacking her as well. He must have gained some confidence while bullying me. She said if he didn't settle down, his days were numbered and that she felt bad about what I'd endured. Now she understood firsthand.

After Janet carried the broom to her chicken yard for a week, Rocko faced his last battle. Janet won, and I felt bad for him. He just thought he was doing his job protecting the hens. However, Rocko had become not only a nuisance but a danger. No one could enter the chicken yard without being attacked. Still, I had hoped for a better outcome.

Several days later Janet asked me to stop by because she had something to show me. When I arrived, she took me down to the chicken yard. My first instinct was to look for Rocko and grab the broom! I laughed to myself even though a part of me felt sad that he was gone. Still, it was a relief to not have to dodge a charging rooster.

Janet motioned me to a small pen with wire all around it. Inside was a chicken who had her wings spread out, and I saw movement under them. Then I saw four, five...no, six tiny chicks! I squealed with excitement. I'd never seen baby chicks with their mom before. She was keeping them warm.

Wow, I thought. *They really do gather their chicks under their wings to protect them.* Inside I was smiling and talking to the Lord: *I get it, God. It's just like You say in Your Word: You long to gather us like a mother hen and protect us. And You protected me from Rocko each day, even though I had entered a battlefield without Your guidance.*

Janet commented that these chicks were Rocko's offspring; he'd been the only rooster around. I felt somewhat comforted. Rocko had left his mark even though his life had been shortened.

I continued to sit for Janet and her chickens over the next couple of years. One of Rocko's offspring grew up to be a rooster too. Thankfully, he didn't inherit Rocko's disposition, and I never needed that broom again.

Dear Lord, how can I ever thank You for all the times You've protected me—even times I didn't know I was in danger? Your Word says You protect Your children coming and going. Forgive me when I've stepped into enemy territory without Your guidance, but even then You watched over me. Whenever I step away from You, help me to hear Your voice. I'm grateful that You long to gather me under Your protective wings like a hen gathers her chicks. In Your precious Son's name I pray, amen.

4

THE LOST
AND FOUND

~~~~~~~~~

When I am afraid, I put my trust in you.

Psalm 56:3 niv

No relationship can be meaningful without trust, and it's no less important in our relationships with animals. A high-strung Australian shepherd named Zinnia (pronounced Zen-ee-a) had huge trust issues, and she would put my own trust issues to the test when I sat for her while her family was on vacation.

I, too, have an Australian shepherd. Her name is Bella, and she's the most loyal and trusting dog I've ever owned. As a breed, Australian shepherds are extremely loyal to their families. They also need to have every situation under control at all times. That's why they're amazing herd dogs.

But this wonderful trait can also be a detriment. Some of these dogs distrust anyone who isn't part of their "pack," and they can be so loyal to their families that they'll go to extreme lengths to be near them.

One day I received a call from Zinnia's owner, Sue. I listened attentively as she told me Zinnia didn't allow anyone other than her family members to pet her or come near her. At times, she would be aggressive with strangers, and she became extremely fearful and experienced anxiety whenever her family left her home alone. Because of all this, the family had never taken a real vacation.

Sue asked me to visit so I could meet Zinnia and the rest of the family—and hear their plan. She hoped the plan would make it possible for me to pet-sit while the family took a long-awaited two-week vacation.

As I drove to the family's home on a hot August afternoon, I followed the directions I'd written down. But I missed the last left turn into their neighborhood. Fortunately, I had given myself enough time to get lost because I don't have the best sense of direction. Anyone who knows me can attest to that! (Truth be told, I have *no* sense of direction.) No matter how many times I make mental notes of landmarks or try to memorize street names, I end up somewhere other than my intended destination.

Frustrated, I looked for a place to turn around. A small white church caught my eye, and the sign in front read "Grace Church." I'd seen a sign pointing the way to that church before on a nearby busy street. Almost by reflex, I started singing "Amazing Grace" under my breath. Something about that word—*grace*—settled in my spirit. I made a quick right-hand turn into the parking lot, turned around, and headed toward my destination. Thankfully, I still arrived on time.

The family lived in a quiet neighborhood, and I saw two young girls playing with a dog in their huge front yard. That had to be Zinnia. Sue and her husband, Rob, were also in the yard, ready to greet me. As we made our introductions, Zinnia stood close to Meg, the older of the two girls.

Zinnia was beautiful. She was on the small side, like my Bella. She had a beautiful red-and-tan coat with white splotches that looked almost like freckles. This coloring is known as merle. Her eye color also matched the red coloring in her coat. I sensed Zinnia's nervousness as I followed her family to the front porch and we all sat down on the concrete steps.

Sue told me more about Zinnia's separation anxiety, which was so severe that the family couldn't go anywhere unless Sue's mother-in-law, Angela, could dog-sit. Angela had been in Zinnia's life since she was a puppy, so the dog considered her a member of the immediate family. But Angela was older now, and she struggled to care for Zinnia, especially if the family needed to be away for more than a few hours.

Zinnia's family wanted to work toward getting her accustomed to someone over a period of a few weeks before their vacation. That way, it wouldn't be like leaving her with a stranger. I thought this was a wonderful plan, and it showed me how much they loved their dog and wanted her to feel at ease while they were away.

Sue and Rob asked me to visit a couple of times a week and spend about an hour with Zinnia. If all went as hoped, their pet would start to feel comfortable with me, making for a seamless transition when the family left.

During that first meet and greet, I already tried to get Zinnia to feel more comfortable with me. I played fetch with her, which she loved more than any dog I knew. The family said she would play for hours if her human partner was up to the task.

Zinnia and I played fetch for about 15 minutes, with her family standing close by. I tossed a blue ball across the yard over and over, and she faithfully brought it back to me each time. I was so excited; I felt like she and I were already becoming friends, and every time she brought the ball to me, I praised her.

I decided my time with Zinnia had gone much better than I'd anticipated. However, while Zinnia accepted my compliments, she didn't want me to touch her.

Before I left, I scheduled several return visits, and then I said goodbye to a hopeful family and a dog who stood close by with a slimy blue ball in her mouth.

Despite the early success, I was still nervous about winning this dog's trust. What if I failed? What if the family couldn't take their planned vacation? In all my years of pet-sitting, I had never worried about an animal trusting me. That trust always seemed to come so easily for me. But this situation felt different. There was a lot riding on my success...or failure.

Leaving Zinnia's quiet neighborhood, I came to the traffic light at the intersection of the street I had missed earlier. There, on the other side of the street, was the sign with an arrow pointing left to Grace Church. I smiled to myself and thought that no one would ever miss the location of that little church. I said a quick prayer, asking God for the grace to help me overcome Zinnia's trust issues.

A week later, as I headed to Zinnia's house for another visit, I envisioned how I would approach her and tried to think of ways to gain her trust. This time I didn't miss my turn because I had Grace Church as a landmark. In fact, that church became a landmark for all of my subsequent visits. More important, the church and its sign were reminders that God was always with me no matter what challenges lay ahead.

I pulled into the family's driveway and saw that Rob was waiting on the front porch with Zinnia. He greeted me at the bottom of the steps, handed me the blue ball, and left. I just stood there, a little stunned. Then I glanced at Zinnia, who was anxiously watching her owner walk away.

Don't miss a step, I told myself. Confident, I waved the ball in front of Zinnia and said, "Let's go, girl!" I threw the ball across the yard, and she immediately ran after it. Then she picked it up and brought it to me. As soon as I took it from her, she gave me a panicked look and headed for the backyard, where she'd seen Rob go moments before.

All of my confidence gushed away. I called her name and ran after her, and when I rounded the side of the house, I spotted her at Rob's side. He gave me a consoling smile, and then we all walked to the front yard. I threw the ball once more, but this time Zinnia took it to Rob.

This scene repeated itself over and over in the next three weeks. Zinnia would fetch the ball for me once, but then when we made eye contact, she'd act as though we were meeting for the first time. She'd run away to a safe spot or find one of her family members. I wasn't making any progress with her.

Why didn't she remember all the time I'd spent with her? Why was she still so afraid to trust me? Unfortunately, I knew deep down that Zinnia and I were very much alike.

God knew it too.

Like me, Zinnia wavered between trust and fear. She could trust me for a short time, but as soon as she realized her family had disappeared from view, she would run, frantic, to find them. For a dog, trust doesn't come naturally. And it's the same for us humans. But we have the ability to take steps of faith, doing the exact thing we sometimes find so difficult: trusting the only One who can heal our fears.

I wondered why Zinnia couldn't do that too. Why couldn't she see I was trustworthy? Why couldn't she see I meant her no harm, only good? Why couldn't she trust my love for her? If only she would trust me, everything would be okay.

At that moment, I heard God. He was asking me the same questions.

I was like Zinnia fetching her ball. As long as I was following my routine, everything was fine. But as soon as I felt out of my comfort zone, fear came and trust left. Instead of keeping my eyes on the One who can be trusted, I would run, frantic, looking for anyone or anything that made me feel better. I didn't want to have to step out in faith. I was afraid to trust. I just wanted to get to a familiar place of comfort.

❧

I knew I had to be patient with Zinnia, just as God has always been patient with me. She had never trusted anyone outside of her family. But I was feeling increasing pressure as the family's vacation quickly approached. I asked Sue and Rob if I could add a couple more visits over the next two weeks, and they agreed.

One day when Zinnia and I were playing ball (this time in the backyard), she brought the ball back to me and then did something amazing. She sat at my feet and looked me right in the eyes. She didn't run away. She didn't have that *I have never seen you before in my life* look either! She just waited for me to throw the ball again. With cautious optimism, I did.

She brought it back and sat at my feet once more. For the next 30 minutes, Zinnia played fetch with me, and I was elated. Afterward, she let me pet her. I couldn't wait to share the news with her family.

I had a few more visits scheduled, and each time we made more progress. Zinnia allowed me to pet her at times, and after we played fetch, I sat on the front porch steps where she would sometimes sit next to me. However, just when I thought I had broken through her fear, she would snap at me.

While I was busy building my relationship with Zinnia, Rob was busy building an enclosure around the backyard so Zinnia could have the run of the inside of the house *and* space outside. The hope was that this arrangement would keep her comfortable between my twice-daily visits while the family was on vacation.

Rob completed the enclosure and secured all of the nooks and crannies a few days before they were scheduled to leave. This gave Zinnia time to get used to the new setup and feel comfortable using her new doggy door. Everything seemed to be falling into place as the big day approached.

I felt so good about the progress I had made with Zinnia. Even though it had taken much longer than I'd hoped, she was finally feeling comfortable with me. She came when I called her, and she stayed with me while I sat on the front steps after our playtime was over. Zinnia's family felt confident they could leave her in my care. They also arranged for Angela to come once a day, knowing it would comfort the dog to see another familiar face.

I was scheduled to visit Zinnia the evening of the first day of the family's vacation, and I planned to play ball with her for a while and then feed her dinner. As I drove that familiar path to Zinnia's house, I knew so much hinged on the trust I had gained with her. I was proud of Zinnia for allowing herself to get close to someone who had been a total stranger just a few weeks ago. Most of all, I was grateful to God for helping me with this challenge. I felt confident about the progress we'd made, and I thought everything was going to be fine.

Zinnia excitedly greeted me at the door, but it was obvious by the look on her face that I wasn't who she was expecting. She immediately ran to another room and started barking. I followed her and called her name, speaking gently as had become my practice, but she continued to bark, and she wouldn't let me near her.

This was not what I'd expected.

Then she growled at me, and the fear and mistrust in her auburn eyes tore at my heart.

It's hard to describe my feelings that day, but I imagine I felt the way God must feel when the ones He loves so deeply have forgotten all the times He's brought them through a tough journey and proved Himself trustworthy.

God brought the Israelites out of captivity in Egypt and then parted the Red Sea, making a dry path to safety (Exodus 14:21). But later the people forgot what He'd done, and they stopped trusting Him. They allowed fear to take root in their hearts because they took their eyes off Him. They made idols out of gold and sank back into their comfort zone.

How many times have I done the same? Yet, again, God is always patient. And Zinnia still needed me to be patient too.

I slowly walked toward the kitchen and tried to ignore her incessant barking and growling. I wanted to get her ball and entice her to come outside, but I feared if we played in the front yard, she'd take off and I'd never get her back. As Zinnia watched my every move, I picked up the ball sitting on the kitchen counter, and she quieted down and started for the front door. *Should I take the chance and let her out front?* I wondered. *Dear Lord, please don't let her run away.*

"Are you ready, girl?" I said calmly as I followed her. She shot me a look and then looked back at the door. I opened it and held my breath. Fear shot through my body. I felt as though I'd just leaped off a cliff. Zinnia zoomed out the door as I called out, "Let's play!" and hoped she wouldn't run off.

She stayed on the porch, her tail wagging as excitement replaced the fear in her eyes. I threw the ball, my heart thumping so hard I could almost hear it. The dog's nails made a scratching sound as she dived off the concrete steps. Then she retrieved the ball and dropped it at my feet on the porch. I quickly threw it again because I didn't want to give her time to let fear take over.

Each time I threw the ball, she ran after it and brought it right back. We played for about half an hour. Then I threw the ball one last time and sat down on the front porch steps, just as I had during our training. I didn't want to change the routine, giving Zinnia a reason to panic.

I called to her and waited for her to come sit with me. She stopped a few feet away, holding the ball in her mouth. I could tell she was contemplating her next move. Finally, she climbed the porch steps and stood beside me, dropping the slimy ball on my leg.

"Good girl," I said in a calming, gentle voice. "Such a good girl." I chose not to pet her. Instead, I rose and opened the door, praying she would follow me inside.

She did.

I could tell her nervousness was returning, but I ignored the urge to pet her. I filled her food bowl in the kitchen, but then I left it on the counter and went to sit on the couch. I wanted to give Zinnia a chance to cool down from all the exercise before feeding her, so I called her and patted the cushion beside me, hoping she would sit with me.

I was relieved when, a few seconds later, Zinnia jumped onto the couch and cautiously sat next to me. Slowly, she laid her head on my lap, and I petted her and spoke to her. She looked up at me, and I realized I was no longer seeing fear; I was seeing sadness.

I knew Zinnia understood that her family had left, and that in her mind, they might not be returning. She must have watched them pack up the car. Then everyone drove away, leaving her behind. As much as I wanted to tell her that her family would be back soon, I knew it was impossible for her to understand that. All I could do was comfort her. But no matter how hard I tried, I could never fill her family's shoes.

I was providing little comfort—maybe none at all.

Some dogs stop eating when they're upset, but Zinnia ate all of her food. I was relieved. Then it was time for me to go, but my heart hurt for her. I wondered how she was going to do all by herself, but I already knew. I walked toward the door, trying to avoid looking Zinnia in the eyes. I couldn't bear to see the sadness staring back.

I've seen those sad looks many times when I've left other pets. Most of the time, I think I'm sadder than they are, but I wasn't this time. I knew the sadness in Zinnia was deep. I knew she felt she had been abandoned. Worse, she had been left with someone she didn't fully trust.

As I closed the front door behind me, leaving Zinnia to herself, I couldn't hold back tears. I wanted to take her home with me. But I knew that would only make matters worse; she would still miss her family but in completely unfamiliar surroundings.

I felt as if I'd been punched in the stomach as I drove away in the dark.

The next morning, I visited Zinnia's home as early as possible. I hadn't slept well the night before. I'd even had to resist the urge to get up in the middle of the night and go check on her.

As I turned the key in the front door lock, I sighed gratefully as I heard barking and then saw Zinnia through a window. I was so happy to see her.

But she wasn't as happy to see me. She gave me the same panicked look I had grown so accustomed to, and then she ran away into another room. *At least she's okay*, I thought.

This visit was almost like the one the night before. I was able to get Zinnia to play ball, but she seemed distracted. She seemed to be in a daze, and I sensed a certain preoccupation in her. Later, I sat on the couch with her and tried again to comfort her. She laid her head on my lap and allowed me to pet her for a little while. I knew we had formed a bond. But compared to the bond she had with her family, ours was weak.

Then, just as I started to think she was getting a little better, she bit my hand before jumping off the couch and running off.

I knew she wanted to trust me, but she couldn't because her heart was so burdened with the thought that her family wasn't coming home. I could sense desperation building inside her—that preoccupation I had been sensing was about to come to fruition.

I left that morning with the hope that my evening visit would find Zinnia in a better state of mind. Sometimes it takes even the most confident pets a few days to adjust to their families being away. Perhaps this would be the case with Zinnia.

But as I drove out of her neighborhood, a deep sense of failure blanketed me, and a huge knot formed in both my stomach and my heart. The thought of so many more days like this was heart-wrenching. If Zinnia didn't improve soon, I planned to call Sue and Rob and let them know. I didn't want to interrupt their vacation, but I didn't want Zinnia to suffer either.

That afternoon I received a frantic call from Angela. She had gone to the house to check on Zinnia again, and the dog was missing. She'd clawed a big hole in the containment area Rob had built and run away. My heart stopped. I had been afraid Zinnia would do something like this if given a chance.

I told Angela I would be right over to help her look for Zinnia. I don't even remember the 20-minute drive. Everything was a blur as desperate thoughts ran through my mind. I was so disappointed in myself. *Dear Lord, how will we find her? What if something has happened to her? This is all my fault. I should never have taken this job.* I felt completely hopeless.

I thought about how difficult it had been for Zinnia to trust me. She would try, but then she'd retreat to her comfort zone. At that moment, I knew God had to be *my* comfort zone. I knew this was the time I had to trust Him unwaveringly.

❧

When I am afraid, I put my trust in you (Psalm 56:3 NIV).

I've seen God move in my life in miraculous ways so many times. And I have *never* known Him to forsake me. Ever. In the darkest of times, He has been there. I may not have always felt Him, but He was there through it all.

Yet, like Zinnia, at times I seemed to forget that God had never let me down. And when a new challenge surfaced in my life, the fear came, and trusting was hard.

❧

A lost Zinnia was counting on me to find her, and even if she didn't trust me fully, I wasn't going to let her down.

When I pulled into the driveway, Angela ran out to meet me, distressed. She had driven the entire neighborhood, calling Zinnia's name, but found no trace of her. I offered to look while she stayed at the house in case Zinnia returned.

As I backed onto the street in front of the house, I thought about how this neighborhood had seemed so quiet and peaceful until this moment. Now it felt cold and intimidating. I pulled into a cul-de-sac just one street away and got out of my car. The cul-de-sac faced a large, wooded area. I walked to the end of the asphalt and called Zinnia's name over and over as I looked out into the deep woods.

Part of me thought she would come running out of those woods and then my lesson in trust would be over. But I heard nothing in those woods. All was quiet. Never have I hated the quiet quite like I did then.

I stood there for a few minutes, waiting. I had no idea where to look next. I got back into my car and prayed: *Dear Lord, I don't know where to look for this dog. She could be anywhere. But You know exactly where she is. I don't know how I'll ever find her. Please, please help me. I'm scared. I need Your help. Please direct my path.*

I can't say I felt peace at that moment, but I felt hope as I drove around the neighborhood. It was late afternoon, and I found myself behind a school bus stopped to let some children out. I didn't want my search to be delayed. *Oh Lord, I don't have time to be sitting behind school buses. Can't You move this one out of my way?* But God's timing is *always* perfect.

Finally, the school bus turned down a street I had already searched, and I drove up and down every remaining street in the neighborhood, calling for Zinnia out the window. But she was nowhere to be found. My choices were to drive around the area a second time or go to the main intersection of the busy street at the neighborhood's entrance. I chose the latter.

When I got there and stopped at the red traffic light, I looked to my left and then to my right. *Which way, God? Which way?*

I had sat at that traffic light many times, and I spotted the simple little sign pointing the way to Grace Church. The arrow under the words pointed left. At that moment, I heard a familiar, quiet whisper: *Go left.*

The light turned green, and I turned left.

My heart sank a little because this was such a busy road. I feared if Zinnia had made it all the way out here, she might have been hit by a car. I drove slowly, looking around as I prayed I wouldn't spot her lying in the street.

Then as I neared Grace Church, I glanced into its parking lot, and a movement caught my eye. I looked closer. It was Zinnia, erratically running back and forth. I had already passed the entrance, so I had to find a place to turn around. I was afraid she'd be gone before I could get back to the church, so since not a single other vehicle was on this usually busy street, I made a U-turn right there in the middle of it. I didn't want to waste precious time.

"Thank You, God!" I shouted.

I pounded the steering wheel anxiously as I drove back to the church parking lot. But when I got there, she was gone. I jumped out of my car. "Zinnia! Zinnia!" I called over and over, scanning the entire area. How could she have vanished so quickly? I choked back tears. I had just missed her.

But then I spotted some movement off to one side of the church, and Zinnia came bounding up an embankment. She stopped when she saw me, and when she started running toward me, I ran toward her!

"Zinnia! Come here, girl!" I cried. I could see the look of complete relief, not fear, in her eyes. She knew me. She trusted me. As soon as we met in the middle, I grabbed her and held her like I'd never held anything in my life! She was wet, and her paws were full of mud, but I carried her to my car and put her in the front seat. No way was I giving her a chance to run again.

But I could tell she didn't want to run away. She nuzzled me and stood on the console of my car, trying to get onto my lap and smearing mud onto my shirtsleeve. I cried, and I thanked God. What a miracle to have found her! What a miracle that she was safe after crossing that busy road. What a miracle that God had brought her to a church that had been such a significant part of my journey over the past month or so.

I called Angela and could barely get the words out. "I found her!"

Angela was incredulous. "Where?"

"At Grace Church, about two miles from her house." Angela was doubly shocked because I had found her that far away.

As I pulled into the driveway, Angela ran to meet us. We carried Zinnia into the house together, not taking any chances she might bolt again. Angela had already called Sue and Rob. Sue had been distraught when she learned Zinnia had clawed out of her enclosure, but now she was relieved and ecstatic that we'd found her. We all were.

Looking back, I realize Zinnia had gone to look for her family, to find her comfort zone. A loyal Australian shepherd, she was determined to go to extreme lengths to find them. But now that she was home and her family was still missing, what were Angela and I going to do? What if Zinnia ran away again?

Everyone decided that Zinnia needed to stay inside the house unless Angela or I was with her, so we closed off her access to the outside world except when she was on a leash. Angela decided to make two or three visits in between my morning and evening visits so Zinnia wouldn't have to spend so many hours alone during the remaining days of her family's vacation.

In the days following Zinnia's escape, I sensed our bond growing stronger. But because I was worried about her running off again, we now played ball in the house. Fortunately, the home had a huge great room with plenty of space. I also took her on frequent walks, and we spent quiet time together on the couch.

Zinnia was still sad, of course. But I knew her family would be back soon, and then her heart would be at ease once more.

When the family returned, Sue called to tell me that Zinnia was beyond excited to see them. She sent me a picture of Zinnia sitting with Meg, and I could see the relief in the dog's eyes. She was back in her comfort zone now, but she had learned an important lesson: She could trust someone beyond her immediate family. Otherwise, she never would have come to me that day in the church parking lot.

And if Zinnia could learn to trust, so could I.

About a week later, I received the nicest note from Sue. She thanked me for all I had done for Zinnia—especially for finding her when she ran away. She added that they'd decided not to plan another long vacation, and that made me happy for Zinnia.

I've thought of Zinnia often over the years. Despite the huge challenge caring for her was, I will always love her, and she will always be special to me. I'll never forget the miracle God did that day when a lost dog taught me about trust and brought us both to a place called Grace.

Dear Lord, I can never thank You enough for all the times You've been faithful to me. I know You've been patient with me when I've forgotten those times and let my fear replace my trust. Thank You for helping me find Zinnia that day. I know it was only through Your amazing grace that I found her. Thank You for teaching me to trust You more fully, and for helping me see that You are my only true Comfort Zone. In Jesus's name, amen.

5

SHILOH'S PROMISE

He brought them out of darkness,
the utter darkness, and broke away their chains.

PSALM 107:14 NIV

One of the hardest things for me to come to terms with is seeing or hearing about animals that have been abused or neglected. I can't bear even the thought of one of God's beautiful creatures being subjected to human cruelty. It baffles me beyond words, and it angers me even more.

I long for the day when the Lord returns and rectifies all of the wrongs in our fallen, hostile world. But if I can help an animal escape from a life of pain and neglect now, my prayer is the same as young Isaiah's: "Here am I! Send me" (Isaiah 6:8).

One day in early June, I was contacted by Amos, a horse trainer who needed my services to care for his horses while he was away at a training clinic. Amos and I had never met, but my horse veterinarian had recommended me. I scheduled a meeting to discuss what the job entailed before I committed to it, though. Not only had I never cared for multiple horses at the same time, but I knew it would be a big job.

Amos's farm was just a few miles from my home—a plus. When I arrived, I drove down a winding, grassy path to the barn, where we'd planned to meet. His place was small yet included a huge training arena and lots of green pasture. The arena was to the right of the barn, and it had several training barrels strategically placed around it. I also noticed a huge pasture on my left and counted five horses grazing there. They popped up their heads as I drove by and then went back to devouring grass by the mouthful.

I pulled into a parking area in front of the small, rustic barn, got out of my car, and looked around for Amos. The temperature was pleasant, and the humidity that usually accompanies June in Georgia hadn't yet made its presence known. I was grateful because there's nothing fun about cleaning a horse stall on a hot, humid day.

I heard the sound of boots crunching on the gravel behind me, and as I turned around I heard a voice say, "Are you Christi?"

I smiled and extended my hand to a man wearing Wranglers and a gray cowboy hat. "I'm Amos," he said in a confident, horse-trainer kind of way. We exchanged small talk for a few minutes, and then he showed me the barn and explained what my duties would be for the three days he planned to be away.

Just as I expected, this would be a huge job. Amos would be taking two of his seven horses with him, but two other horses would be there as well as his other five because others trained in the arena. That meant I'd be caring for seven horses. But I love being around horses. I have three of my own, and I rarely turn down a chance to care for *any* horse.

I agreed to take the job, and Amos was appreciative. It's hard to find someone you can trust to take care of horses. Not many people know that much about them, let alone can handle the physical, financial, and emotional demands of caring for them. There's so much more to it than just throwing feed in a bucket and filling a water trough, yet too many people buy a horse and then find themselves in an expensive predicament because they didn't have a thorough knowledge of the dynamics of horse care. Unfortunately, the horse is the one that usually suffers in that situation. Horses may look strong and resilient, but they can be fragile and extremely sensitive to so many elements.

Amos took good care of his horses. He worked them hard, but he rewarded them generously. Each horse's stall was immaculate, and they all had the best feed and hay. (My horses have much the same situation—except they don't see much hard work! To a horse trainer like Amos, my horses are considered spoiled. But that's a different story...)

The three days I cared for Amos's horses came and went without any problems. I was glad the job wasn't longer, though. It was exhausting, and by the third day, I was glad to be finished with it.

I had been thinking about buying another horse for myself, though, and I thought Amos might be a good resource to help me find one. My husband had a good trail horse, but because I didn't have one, he and I did little riding together. When Amos returned from his trip, I asked him if he knew of any possibilities.

He offered to do some research and ask around. He knew a lot of people in the horse world and, at that time, horses were plentiful because so many people were having financial difficulties. Some owners were even giving their horses away, but I'd heard about others dumping their horses in the woods, abandoning them in other people's pastures, and far worse.

A couple of days later, Amos told me he knew of a horse for sale. He didn't know a lot about the horse; the owner, Lee, was just someone he knew of through the grapevine. But he'd been told that the horse was about 12 years old, a gelding (male), and an excellent trail horse. He sounded perfect for what I was looking for.

I agreed to take a look at the horse, and Amos arranged to have Lee bring him to his training facility so I could ride him in the arena. Amos also agreed to evaluate the horse's capabilities for me and give me his opinion on his temperament and other attributes.

When I arrived, Amos was already in the arena with the horse, who was saddled up. Lee had dropped the horse off and left.

I walked to the gate of the arena and stood with my arms hanging over its top board. As Amos walked the horse over from the far end of the arena, which was about 40 feet away, I noticed the gelding's lanky conformation. He was tall—probably about 16.5 hands, which is quite tall for a horse. As Amos drew closer, I realized this horse was not just "lanky" but quite thin. I didn't say anything right then, but I pulled the latch on the gate and walked inside.

"Hey, boy," I said as I stroked his nose. He threw his head up a little, and Amos gave him a quick, gentle yank with the reins. He was a chestnut color with a wide, white blaze down the length of his face and four white pasterns on his legs.

"He's a little thin," Amos said as I walked down the side of the horse's body, running my hand the length of it. "Take him for a trot around the arena." Amos handed me the reins, and I placed my foot in the stirrup and swung my leg up. That was a high mount, and I was surprised I was able to do it! None of my horses have ever been taller than 15 hands.

By the way my legs hung down around the horse's body, I could tell he was even thinner than I'd thought. I walked him around the arena a couple of times and then trotted him. It was rough ride.

It's always strange at first when you get on a horse you're not used to riding, but this just felt off. I dismounted, and when I walked around to the front of the horse, I noticed his nostrils were flaring in and out as though he was out of breath.

"He's more than a 'little thin,'" I said as Amos walked up beside us.

He kicked into the ground with the point of his boot. "He is, but I'd never met the owner before today, so I don't know too much about the situation."

"What's his name?" I asked.

"Lee said it's Dakota."

I asked Amos to take off the saddle so I could get a really good look at Dakota's condition, which was mostly covered up by the long blanket under the saddle.

Amos removed both the saddle and blanket, and I was shocked. Under all that tack was a terribly emaciated horse!

Amos shot me a look that told me he knew exactly what I was thinking. "Yeah. I had no idea he was this thin. He was saddled up when Lee took him off the trailer this morning." He wiped the palms of his hands down the front of his jeans.

"My goodness! What on earth?" I exclaimed. "Didn't he say anything about this?" Amos shook his head. This was why Dakota's gate felt so off and the ride felt so rough. He barely had the energy to walk let alone hold a rider on his back and trot. As I looked closer at his entire body, every rib was visible and every bone in his pelvis protruded with only skin covering it. His body was covered with scars—everywhere.

I had never seen a horse in this condition in person, only on those television commercials about animal abuse and neglect. Now it was authentic and tangible, and it stared me in the face.

I wanted to scream. I felt horrible that I had made him carry me on his back and trot. Amos and I stood silent as thoughts raced through my mind. This was not a horse I could buy as a trail horse—at least not when he was in this shape. But I wanted to know his story. Why was he so thin? Why was his owner selling him?

As I looked into Dakota's eyes, I could see his immediate story. He was frightened. He was tired. He was unsure of what was going to happen next. His eyes were wide, and his eyelids furrowed and wrinkled in a way that gave him a look of concern. It broke my heart.

I had not been prepared to see this situation, let alone have to carry the burden on my heart. This hurt.

I told Amos this horse was not what I was looking for. He knew that, of course. Dakota needed a *lot* of care and a *lot* of food to get him in any kind of decent shape. It would take at least a year to get some decent weight on him. I estimated he needed to gain a good 400 pounds, and given his current condition, there was a good chance he had other health problems as well.

I shook my head as I turned and opened the arena gate to leave. I thanked Amos for setting up the meeting and asked him to keep his eyes open for any other horses. Then I watched him walk Dakota over to a holding pen. Without the saddle and blanket covering the top half of his body, I could see his hip bones were even more prominent and that his hind end was nothing but skin and bones.

I got into my car, and the anger and sadness over what I had just witnessed came pouring out. As I pulled out of the parking area and drove down the grassy road leading out of the property, I could barely see through the blur of tears. I felt sick. I cried all the way home, my emotions flopping back and forth from deep sadness to raging anger. Who could let a beautiful creature like Dakota waste away like that? What state of mind must a human be in to ignore his obvious condition? It just didn't make sense. Was there something medically wrong with him? If that was the case, why didn't Lee mention it?

I just couldn't comprehend what I had just witnessed.

When I arrived home, my husband met me in the driveway. As the tears continued to flow, I told him every detail of what had transpired at Amos's facility. He shook his head. He, too, couldn't fathom what had led to Dakota's condition.

That evening, I kept going over and over what I had seen earlier that day, and I couldn't get the look in Dakota's big brown eyes out of my head. It was etched deep in both my mind and my heart.

I woke up several times during the night and shook my husband's shoulder, waking him with questions: "Can't we just buy Dakota and keep him until we can find him a home?" Then, "What if I get the vet out and have her check him over? Then if he's healthy, can't we just feed him, get him back in shape, and make him my trail horse?"

Each time my husband answered in his half-sleep state, "Whatever you want to do."

"I want to go get him!" I said with conviction as I turned over for the last time until morning.

As the light of day seeped through our bedroom window, I sprang out of bed and ran to the kitchen. When I grabbed my cell phone and dialed Amos's number, surprisingly, he answered. I had just glanced at the clock on the stove and realized it was 6:00 a.m. I apologized for the early call, but Amos said he was always up by 5:30 anyway.

I told him I wanted to look into purchasing Dakota and have a vet look at him before I determined my next steps.

I could tell Amos was surprised by the somewhat puzzled tone in his voice. But he said he'd contact Lee, find out what he would be willing to do, and call me back. Within just a few minutes, he did. Lee was willing to bring Dakota to my house and give me a couple of days to have him checked out. A huge weight lifted from my shoulders. If I could get Dakota home with me, he'd be safe and cared for. I wouldn't have to worry about him anymore.

My husband set up a temporary pen for him in front of our barn because I was a little concerned about having him too close to my other horses in case he had any health issues. But it was a nice grassy area and a perfect spot for me to watch him from the house.

That very day a small, dilapidated horse trailer pulled into our driveway. It was covered in rust spots and looked as if it was going to fall apart at any moment. A thin man wearing a baseball cap got out of a white pickup, and I greeted him with a handshake. His demeanor was rough, but he was pleasant as he filled me in.

He had owned Dakota for about ten months, and his sister-in-law had just ridden him on a three-hour trail ride a couple of days ago. He went on to tell me what a great trail horse he was. I bit my tongue, holding back judgmental words, but no one should have been riding that horse for three minutes let alone three hours in the condition he was in.

He also said he'd been working on getting weight on him, but no matter how hard he tried, Dakota never gained any. I asked him about Dakota's history, but he said he could only tell me that he got him from a friend of a friend.

He wanted $400 for him. That wasn't a lot for a horse, but it was a lot for a horse in Dakota's condition, especially in the current economy. But I was careful not to react, and I asked if he could go ahead and get Dakota off the trailer.

I watched as he stepped inside the trailer and, taking the lead rope, led the horse backward. He handled him in a somewhat frustrated manner that made me uneasy. And then after Dakota stepped back and down off the trailer and the man turned him to face me, I was horrified. Fresh blood was streaming down Dakota's face, and my eyes were drawn to a huge gash between his eyes.

"What happened?" I asked in an urgent tone, my volume causing Dakota to throw his head. I immediately placed my hand gently on his nose.

"I'm sorry, boy," I said as I gave Lee a demanding look. I did not have a good feeling about this man. I had given him the benefit of the doubt about Dakota's condition and weight, but I wasn't letting him off the hook about this.

"Some lady driving in front of me slammed on her brakes, and I had to stop really fast," he said. "His head must have hit the front of the trailer."

Anger burned inside of me. I know accidents can happen, but I wasn't buying it. Still, I held my words, and taking the lead from the man, I led Dakota to the pen, where I had already set up with hay and water for him. Lee followed close behind, rattling on about what a good horse Dakota was. But none of that mattered at this point. I didn't care about anything he had to say. My deepest gut feeling told me something about this whole situation wasn't right.

I put Dakota in the pen and walked back toward the driveway as Lee followed me. "How old is he, again?" I asked.

"His Coggins says he's twelve." He handed me the paperwork. A Coggins test is required for any horse traveling out of state or being sold, as well as for some other instances. It shows a blood test has been done to screen for a disease that's highly contagious in horses and has no cure. It's rare for a horse to be positive, but it does happen. Amos, though, had already checked out Dakota's paperwork, and he didn't have the disease.

I thanked Lee for bringing him and said I'd be in touch with my decision. "Take your time," he said. I tried to be as polite as I could, but all I wanted was for him to leave. As he drove away, I quickly ran into the house for antiseptic solution and towels to clean Dakota's wound.

Back in his pen, I gently cleaned the blood off his face. The gash was deep, and I felt so bad for him. He stood quietly and allowed me to clean it, but his eyes were wide with uncertainty.

"I'm not going to hurt you, boy. I promise." I gently stroked his neck and surveyed him more closely. He had so many scars, and he was so, so thin. The thought of his being made to carry someone on his back for a three-hour trail ride made me sick to my stomach. I had some choice words for that sister-in-law, but I knew it wasn't my place to criticize, especially when I didn't know the entire story.

I went into the barn and got some treats for him, and Dakota gladly took them. Then he ate some of his hay. He seemed calm, but I think that had to do with his being so weak. A well-fed, healthy horse can have a lot of spunk and a lot of energy to act up if it wants to. Dakota just seemed as if he didn't have the energy to be anything but calm and agreeable.

I called my horse veterinarian and asked her to come and evaluate his health. She was able to schedule her visit for the next day.

That evening I spent some time with Dakota and talked to him. I also gently stroked his face and neck, although he definitely evaded my touch, known as being head shy. Yet he seemed to get past that after a while. Horses can be head shy for various reasons, but usually they're frightened because of something that happened to them in the past. Perhaps someone struck him in the face. Or maybe no one ever took the time to get him used to being touched on his face. Either way, it's not positive for a horse to be head shy.

I gave him a couple more treats before I left him for the night.

Once again, I spent wakeful hours thinking about Dakota. What had I done? Had I acted on impulse instead of praying and seeking God's will for this situation? I've brought home many needy animals, but this commitment was much bigger than bringing home a stray kitten or an injured bird. What would I do if Dakota didn't work out? *Oh Lord, what have I done?* I prayed as I tossed and turned.

The next day I was eager for the vet to come. Dakota was underweight, but I held on to the hope that he was otherwise healthy.

When I walked with her to the pen where Dakota was munching on hay, she said, "Wow. He's not in good shape." She checked him from front to back and opened his mouth. "First, he's not 12. He's at the very least 19 or 20." Then she picked up his feet and showed me the hard knobs on his fetlocks. She explained this was a sign of joint damage in horses that have either been used for jumping for many years or are older and have been worked hard. Either way, it's severe, and horses with this condition should never be ridden regularly. She also cautioned against anyone riding him at all in his current condition.

Then she gave me a consoling look and told me this horse was of no use for riding. His best option was to be put out to pasture and spend his last few years doing nothing but grazing. However, he first needed to gain a lot of weight.

This was not what I'd wanted to hear. I had hoped she would tell me all he needed was some good hay and feed and all would be well.

She got into her truck to leave and said she was sorry she didn't have better news, but whoever had this horse before had worked him hard. I waved goodbye, and then I joined Dakota, who watched me as he ate his hay.

"What's your story, boy?" I asked, feeling deflated. He had given his best to someone, and then they'd discarded him when he was no longer of use. Perhaps they had fallen on hard times and had to give him up, but that was of no comfort to me. And looking at Dakota, I was sure it would be of no comfort to him.

We couldn't afford to both keep him and get another trail horse. But the thought of giving him back to Lee ripped at my heart. It was so unfair.

That evening, I told my husband everything I'd learned from the vet, and in his quiet wisdom he confirmed that it wasn't feasible for us to keep Dakota. But it still felt so wrong to send him back to his owner, so I prayed. *If there's any way to find him another home, God, please lead me to it.* Like so many times before, I knew I was asking for a miracle. Anyone who knew anything about horses would never want to buy him.

I walked out to the pen, and he raised his head from grazing as I greeted him. His wide eyes watched me as I stuck my arms through the bars to touch his side. "I'm so sorry I can't keep you. I would give anything to get you away from that man." I opened the gate and slipped inside. Dakota stood quiet and continued to watch me. "I don't know what's going to come about, but I promise you with all my heart that I'm going to get you away from him!" I stroked his nose and eyed the gash on his forehead that was now scabbed over but still visible. I meant that promise; I just didn't know how I would keep it.

I left his pen and walked to the barn to get more treats. By now Dakota knew where the treats were kept and anticipated my bringing him some. He softly nickered and came close to the edge of the pen. I gave him the treats, and as he munched them, I told him once more I would keep my promise.

I dragged myself back to the house, dreading the call I had to make.

I told Lee that the vet's visit had not gone well, and that according to the vet and Dakota's teeth, he was around 20 years old, not 12. I also told him the horse was severely malnourished, and because of his severe joint damage, he shouldn't be ridden—possibly ever again.

The man immediately became argumentative. He said there was no way Dakota was 20 years old and that he'd been riding him just fine ever since he got him. He also disagreed that Dakota was in a malnourished state. He was just naturally thin, he said. He'd fed him well, but he just never put on weight.

I decided not to argue with him; I already knew the truth. And with gut-wrenching words, I said, "I can't buy him."

He said he would be by to pick up Dakota first thing in the morning.

It was a long, long night. I wavered between all the reasons to let him go and trying to come up with ways to keep him. But I knew in the deepest part of my heart, the same place that was so shattered over Dakota, that letting him go was the right decision.

The next morning, I spent as much time as I could with Dakota. I brushed him and cleaned his feet. I doctored his wound one last time. I told him how much I loved him. I reminded him of my promise to somehow get him out of his bad situation. And as I looked into his eyes, I thought he understood.

Lee pulled into the driveway with the same rusty trailer. He was surprisingly pleasant as he carried a halter and lead rope down to Dakota's pen, but when he fastened the halter around his head, the horse threw his head a little.

I could not watch.

The man told me he was sorry it didn't work out and led Dakota out of the pen and through the gate that separated my barn from my driveway. I'll never forget that sight.

Dakota got right in the trailer, and then I watched as it disappeared down the road.

I felt sick the rest of the day. It took everything I had not to call that man and tell him I wanted Dakota back, and I stood staring at that empty pen several times that day.

My heart felt as empty. Each time I thought of Dakota, I prayed. I pleaded with God to somehow work this out. But as much as I wanted to believe He would, I just didn't see how that could happen.

The next day a friend I hadn't known very long dropped by to return something she'd borrowed. Bonnie and I had met in a small-animal vet's office (no surprise there), and we each had several dogs.

Bonnie and her husband, Calvin, also had horses, so we had a lot in common.

When Bonnie saw the pen where Dakota had been, she asked me about it, and I gave her the whole story.

Then she told me she'd just met a lady named Helen in our vet's office the day before (Bonnie obviously spends a lot of time there!) who was there with a puppy. As the two women talked, Bonnie learned that Helen had an older horse and wanted to find another horse to be a friend to him. Bonnie offered to contact Helen to see if she was interested in buying Dakota.

I was awestruck. A part of me thought it wouldn't pan out, and I was ashamed of my lack of faith. But if this was an answer to my prayer, it would be the miracle I'd pleaded with God to give me.

Later that evening Bonnie called to say Helen wanted to speak with me. She gave me her number, and I immediately called her. Helen's horse was 21 years old and named Moonshine. She'd raised him since his birth, and she loved him dearly. But he had just lost his best friend and only pasture-mate the week before, and he was so sad and depressed that he wouldn't eat. He also stood over his best friend's grave in the front of his pasture for hours at a time.

I asked her if she would be interested in taking Dakota to give Moonshine a new friend. She would, but she couldn't afford to pay more than $200 for him. I offered to buy him if, as long as he worked out, she'd agree to keep him for the rest of his life. She did.

As soon as I hung up, I called Lee and told him I had someone interested in buying Dakota. He agreed to let us visit and gave me directions.

The next day Helen and I drove to Lee's place, which was about 25 miles from where I lived. When I picked her up, I realized I had driven by her home nearly every day. She lived only about two miles from me, on a main street I had to travel every time I went anywhere at all.

It was a hot and humid afternoon as we pulled into our destination. The driveway was long and unpaved, and fenced property lined both sides. Because I saw no grass or pasture, I wondered where Dakota could even be kept.

We pulled up to a large house that was almost elegant. The property surrounding it certainly didn't do it justice. And several cars were in the driveway. As Helen and I got out of my car, Lee came to meet us. A lady and a young boy walked part way with him, but then they sat down on the front porch of the house.

When the man said he would take us to where Dakota was, to my surprise he opened a gate that led to the property that lined the left side of the driveway. That's where I'd also seen a couple of rundown sheds, huge rocks, pieces of rusty farm equipment, and a lot of trash strewn about. As Helen and I stepped through the worst of it, I still wondered where a horse would be kept because the area he was leading us through wasn't fit for one. Then I saw Dakota about 30 feet away. He was standing in the middle of a barren pasture that looked more like a dumping ground.

He had on a halter with a long rope tied to a dilapidated shed. "Here he is," Lee said as he went up to Dakota and patted him firmly on the neck. "He's a great horse," he added in his typical sales-pitch fashion. "I'll leave you to look at him for a while, and then you can let me know. But I do want to tell you that another lady and her son are here, and they're interested in him too."

After he left us with Dakota, Helen and I both rolled our eyes. We didn't believe anyone else wanted to buy Dakota, but it didn't matter. Helen wanted him, and that's all I needed to hear. Dakota stood pitifully. There was no hay or shelter for him, and his rope gave him only about 20 feet to roam.

Soon the woman and her son made their way through the trash-laden terrain toward us. She started telling tell me what a beautiful horse he was. "He's a tall drink of water, isn't he?" she said as she ran her hand down the length of his gaunt body. "I rode him the other day, and he's a great trail horse." The young boy nodded his head in agreement as she smiled, and I shot her a half-smile and bit my tongue as I'd been learning to do ever since I first met Lee. I knew full well he had sent her to talk to us in hopes it would spur us on to buying him and paying his ridiculous price.

I just wanted them to go away so Helen and I could talk about our plan to get Dakota out of there. Finally, after several minutes of dead silence from Helen and me, the two slipped away. Helen reminded me she didn't have a horse trailer, but I did, so that wasn't a problem. We agreed to pick up Dakota the very next morning. Neither one of us wanted to leave him there one second longer than we had to.

I gave Dakota one last look before leaving and stroked his soft muzzle. As much as it hurt to see him in those conditions, at least I knew it was for only one more night. I whispered to him, "I told you I would get you out of here. Remember? I promised I would, and I did." I'll never forget the look he gave me. It was a look of relief, and I knew he somehow understood.

Helen and I trekked back through the trash-laden obstacle course, leaving Dakota tied to the broken-down shed that kept him imprisoned in a 20-foot section of hell. Lee was in the driveway waiting for us, and I told him we would come for Dakota the next morning. I gave him a $100 deposit, hoping Dakota would still be there when we arrived.

Relief flowed through me like warm cider on the coldest day of the year. I could hardly believe what had transpired in just over 24 hours! God had given me the miracle I'd asked for. I felt ashamed that I had doubted Him, but between the poor economy and Dakota's poor condition, I thought finding him a home was as close to impossible as me flying home that evening.

Immediately, I was reminded that *nothing* is impossible for God. The impossibilities lie only within our own mistrusting hearts. God is fully able to do above and beyond all that we ask (Ephesians 3:20).

When I told Helen about my prayer and that she was the answer to that prayer, I learned she'd already decided on a new name for Dakota—Shiloh (and now you know why the name Shiloh is in the title of this chapter). Shiloh means "peace." *What a beautiful name for him,* I thought. How fitting, because that's what God was granting him. He would now have peace. He would have that home he deserved, that home I promised him, all glory be to God.

Helen and I picked up Shiloh the next morning. We took him to her house, where she had blocked off a section of pasture just for him. This would give Shiloh and Moonshine a chance to get to know each other over a fence before being put together.

She asked me how long I thought she should keep them separate, and I said about five days. She agreed. However, the very next day she told me Shiloh and Moonshine had stood neck to neck the entire night. So she put them together. At first, I was concerned, but Helen said it was as if they'd been together for a year; they hadn't left each other's side since she opened up the fence. Moonshine no longer stood over his old friend's grave, and he was eating again and acting like himself.

I was so happy.

Shiloh was happy too.

Helen and I kept in touch for a few years after that. Within just a few months, Shiloh had gained a huge amount of weight, and he was beautiful. I also saw him every time I drove by Helen's house. I would see Shiloh and Moonshine grazing together, never more than five feet apart.

He brought them out of darkness, the utter darkness,
and broke away their chains (Psalm 107:14 NIV).

Shiloh's story is much like ours. We're all born into this world bound by the chains of our sin. But a Savior waits patiently to break the chains that keep us imprisoned. He wants to give us a new name and a new life. He is faithful to His promises—always.

Shiloh and Moonshine lived together for about six years. As I was driving past Helen's house one day, I saw Shiloh standing alone in the pasture. I knew his best friend must have passed away because it was the only time I had seen them apart. I called Helen, and she confirmed it. I felt bad for Shiloh, but he lived another two years after that. He'd been given eight wonderful years with Helen, and he deserved every one of them.

It was hard to drive by Helen's after Shiloh passed away because I never got tired of seeing him peacefully grazing in that pasture. But even in its quiet emptiness, that pasture reminded me that God is the Great Deliverer and the Great Promise-Keeper. He rescues us all from the chains that bind us, and He sets us free.

*Dear Lord, what a Great Deliver You are. You
keep all Your promises. You break the chains and*

set the captive free. Thank You for the miracle You did when You found Shiloh a home. Thank You for caring for a horse who was no longer wanted. But You still saw his value, and You see mine as well. Most of all, thank You for setting me free through Your death on a Roman cross. In Jesus's name, amen.

6

PAJAMAS
AT WORK

~~~~~~~~~~~

Delight yourself also in the LORD,
and He shall give you the desires of your heart.

PSALM 37:4

I've never put much effort into planning what to wear. It's not that I don't want to look presentable or that I don't care if my shoes go with my outfit; I just don't want to spend a lot of time putting it all together. Besides, looking good can be uncomfortable.

Honestly, I'd prefer to wear flip-flops and pajamas every day. Before I was blessed with the best job in the world, I was required to wear typical business attire, but I never enjoyed wearing high-heeled shoes, blazers, and, worst of all, dresses! I would jokingly say to coworkers, "Someday I'm going to have a job that lets me wear my pajamas to work!"

Fast-forward about 15 years. God allowed me to leave the corporate world and have that "dream job." And you know what? I wore my pajamas to work many times. Animals are amazing, but most of all, they don't judge. They don't care if your shoes don't match your purse. They don't whisper behind your back if every hair isn't perfectly in place.

Best of all, they're fine if you feed them wearing your pajamas. They're happy with a good belly rub, a tasty treat, and someone who loves them. That's why it was easy to get away with wearing my comfortable clothes when making pet-sitting visits. Only the animals saw me.

Most of the time.

All my first visits of the day were done at an early hour because the animals were eager to be let out and be given something to eat. So one of the great perks of my job as a pet sitter was to roll out of bed, throw on my flip-flops, feed my own dogs and horses, and get out the door by 6:30 a.m. to start my pet-sitting visits—without matching outfits or even brushed hair.

Once my morning visits were complete, I got to come home. Then I'd get dressed before my afternoon and evening visits. It was a flawless routine.

Almost.

One morning I was to make a visit to five cats who belonged to a long-time customer named Gina. Cats are easier than dogs because they don't need a crack-of-dawn visit due to a litter box being available. Because I didn't need to be there shortly after six thirty, I arrived around eight instead.

I had on my usual early-morning attire as I arrived at Gina's. I wore a white T-shirt and blue pajama bottoms with yellow ducks printed all over them, bought a few sizes too big so I'd be comfortable in them. Of course, I'd tied the top drawstring extra tight to take up the extra three or four sizes in the waistband. (Remember, judge-free zone here!) A denim baseball cap covered my head, and, of course, no outfit is complete without flip-flops.

Gina had a steep driveway. Sometimes she and her husband took their car with them on trips, leaving a spot in their garage so I could pull my car into it. But if they left their car in the garage, I had to park on the street at the bottom of the driveway. The driveway was just too steep to park on such an incline.

This time I'd have to park on the street. And if I hurried, I could scale the driveway quickly and slip into the house without being noticed. But even if I was spotted by the occasional neighbor walking a dog or leaving for work, it wouldn't be that big a deal. My pajama bottoms weren't that over the top...unless I'd worn my favorites. They had big black-and-white Dalmatians printed against a bright yellow background.

I parked my car lengthwise across the bottom of the driveway on the street. Then, unfortunately, I spotted several men landscaping the neighbor's yard just to the left of Gina's house. I sighed. *Well,* I thought, *I'll just get out and run up the driveway as fast as I can.* But first I grabbed a pair of sunglasses out of the glove box and put them on so I could inconspicuously survey what the workers were doing.

I counted six men digging, planting, and whatever else they were doing at this inopportune time. *Thank goodness I don't have on my Dalmatian pants,* I thought while taking a deep breath and preparing to make my quick jaunt up the mountainous driveway. Maybe they wouldn't even notice me in their busy pursuit of tearing up the neighbor's yard.

I took one more deep breath, and then I went for it! I opened my car door, got out, and closed it without missing a beat. I decided to cross in front of my car instead of behind it so I wouldn't have to run through the grass to get to the driveway, even though that would put me in perfect view for all to see.

I sprang to the front of my car, never looking to the men on my left, and the most horrible thing happened: My pajama bottoms dropped to my ankles, giving the landscape crew the best seat in the house. If tickets were being sold for that horrifying view, they would have been a thousand dollars each—certainly not the cheap seats!

"Oh my gosh!" I exclaimed. Then in one seamless nanosecond I had my pajama bottoms up and tied back around my waist. Before I knew it, I was at Gina's front door. How I scaled the driveway that rivaled Mount Everest and made it through the front door, I'll never know. It was all an excruciating blur. But there I was, standing in the foyer. Five kitties came running, but I stood frozen.

I don't know if words exist to describe what I was feeling. And only one thing was more terrifying than what had just happened—going back out to my car to leave. With five kitties now purring and winding around my legs, I realized that for the first time ever, I knew the true meaning of the word *speechless*.

I honestly wanted to cry, but that wouldn't have reflected my true emotion. Then I wanted to hide, but that wasn't fitting either. All I could do was laugh—out loud. What else could be done in such a situation? And as I prepared breakfast for Gina's cats I couldn't stop laughing. I laughed the entire time I was there.

Until it was time to leave.

How can I go back to my car after what happened? I asked myself. *There's just no way to recover.* But I gathered my courage—well, I must have borrowed it from someone else because I had none at that moment—and walked out the door. I could feel my face burning as the blood rushed to my cheeks. Each humiliating step to the bottom of the endless driveway felt like a slog through quicksand. I didn't look toward those men one time as I stayed focused on my destination at the bottom for what seemed like an eternity. Then I got in my car and drove away.

Once I got out of Gina's neighborhood, I felt relieved. "Dear Lord," I prayed out loud, "please let them finish that job today before I have to go back again."

When I returned home, I thought about the events leading up to that horrifying moment. Unbeknownst to me, the drawstring to my pajama bottoms had somehow come untied. Because they were a few sizes too big, once I stood up they just dropped to the ground.

That day I told everyone I spoke to about my "incident," and they all had the same reaction—they laughed so hard they cried.

And each time I told the story, I laughed a little more about it. It was funny; I just wished it hadn't happened to me!

When Gina returned from her trip, I told her about it too. She couldn't stop laughing either.

Delight yourself also in the LORD, and He shall give you
the desires of your heart (Psalm 37:4).

As I think back on my wish for a job where I could wear my pajamas to work, I'm reminded once again of God's goodness. He promises us that if we delight in Him, He will give us our deepest desires. Even though that event was horrifying at the time, it made me realize that God had given me exactly what I'd hoped for. But perhaps in all my busyness, I had forgotten.

What does it mean to "delight in the Lord"?

It means that the mere thought of Him brings joy to our hearts. It means that in the darkest of times, we put our trust in Him, knowing He is a God who's trustworthy.

It means no one and no thing are more important to us than He is.

It means our greatest desire is to live for Him.

It means that doing His will becomes our delight.

I may not get that right all of the time, but God is patient, and He is faithful to nudge me along the way if I get off track. I've realized that, as I grow closer to Him, my desires become closer to His desires and doing *His* will becomes the desire of my heart. I think that's exactly what Jesus meant when He said He came to give us abundant life (John 10:10).

I think sometimes we fear we must give up too much to follow

God. But the truth could not be more opposite. That's the lie the enemy wants us to believe. He wants us to think that if we accept God's free gift of salvation, we'll be giving up everything we love in this world. But the truth is we gain everything worth having and we give up only what is not worth having.

I think God has a sense of humor, and that sometimes He reminds me of His goodness and blessings in a not-so-subtle way. I still laugh when I think about that day God reminded me that He had given me the desire of my heart.

Dear Lord, help me never to forget all the desires of my heart You have fulfilled. You are an amazing and good God. Thank You for the blessing of laughter. Bring me to a place where doing Your will becomes my greatest delight and the biggest desire of my heart. In Jesus's name, amen.

7

MOLLY'S EPIPHANY

~~~~~~~

I press toward the goal for the prize
of the upward call of God in Christ Jesus.

Philippians 3:14

I stopped to fluff the pillow on the couch before glancing out my front door's window once more. I was waiting for a potential new customer named Amy to arrive. We'd be discussing the possibility of my boarding her dog, Molly.

Depending on certain factors, many times I would board dogs in my home instead of visiting their homes. It was a great option for customers who wanted their dogs to have more attention or whose dogs had anxiety issues when left alone for long periods of time.

The dogs that came to stay at my house were treated just like my own dogs were. They slept on my bed, had free access to the house, and enjoyed playing outside on our large, fenced-in property. As long as everyone got along, boarding worked out great. I always gave new dogs a period of time to get accustomed to the other dogs, but if any of them didn't play nice, I had an area where they'd be set apart to eat, sleep, and feel safe.

In all the years I was in business, only one dog couldn't seem to get along with everyone else. When she came to stay, she had her own personal suite, and that suited her just fine.

I loved having dogs stay with me. I had four dogs of my own, and it was like having their friends visiting for a few days. Everyone knew each other and got along. During my busiest times, I would have as many as 15 dogs at one time, but I loved every minute of it. And my husband deserved a medal for allowing all those dogs on his bed!

I had strict rules, though. Besides being well-tempered, boarding dogs had to be under 25 pounds. This kept everyone on an even playing field. It also gave everyone at least a small spot on the bed with us. They had to come nice and clean, too—no dirty, smelly dogs allowed. Keeping them that way was a different story, but for the most part, boarding worked out.

I checked out the window once more and saw that a blue SUV had pulled up to the driveway gate. My entire property was fenced, and a gate stretched across the driveway so no dogs could get out and nothing unwanted could get in. I made my way out to the driveway to open it, and as the car pulled past me, a scruffy face peered out the front passenger window.

I closed the gate and walked over to the driver's side just as my potential customer, an older lady, was stepping out.

"Hello," she said. "I'm Amy." Then she extended her hand as she struggled to keep the scruffy dog from jumping out of the car at the same time. I laughed.

"It's nice to meet you. And this must be Molly," I said, reaching to help keep the dog from springing over Amy's shoulder and onto the hard, concrete driveway. Amy turned around and wrapped her arms around Molly before lifting her from the car and setting her on the ground. The medium-sized, silver-and-tan terrier mix took off sniffing the ground and everything else in her path.

Molly was no 25-pound dog, however. I estimated she weighed about 40 pounds. I'd informed Amy of our 25-pound limit on the phone, but either she hadn't heard me or she thought I might not notice.

Other potential customers had missed or ignored my weight limit rule, and after meeting them and their dog, I had turned most of them away. On three occasions, however, I'd let it slide, but only because the dog was so gentle and well behaved that I knew it would fit in just fine.

As Amy talked, I sensed a sadness in her voice. I decided not to say anything just yet about her dog's obvious weight surplus, instead inviting her and Molly inside so I could see how the dog behaved indoors.

We women sat down on the couch, and Molly sat at Amy's feet. I sensed she was quite intelligent; after being around so many animals, it had become easy for me to spot the signs. She was well-behaved too, and I could tell she adored Amy.

Amy told me she'd had Molly for only a few months, and that she was a rescue from a shelter who'd been brought back three different times after being adopted. I immediately wondered why no one seemed to want to keep her. What was wrong with her? I was sad for her, but I was waiting for a bombshell explanation. Perhaps Molly didn't get along with other dogs. Or maybe she was destructive. I asked Amy if she could see any reason the other owners had given her up, but she said Molly had been the perfect dog for her.

Amy also told me that her husband had passed away six months ago, just a few weeks before she'd brought Molly into her home. Molly had been a great comfort to her. Tears welled in Amy's eyes as she shared it would have been almost impossible to be at home alone if it weren't for Molly. My heart broke for her, and I immediately knew why Molly had been returned to the shelter three times. God had set Molly aside for Amy.

I agreed to care for Molly while Amy traveled to see her brother, and we scheduled the exact dates for Molly's stay when Amy called a few days later. Since I would be boarding a few other dogs that same time, I was interested to see how Molly would interact with them. But as I said, if she didn't get along with them, I had a spot where she could have her own space but still get all the attention she needed from me.

Amy dropped off her dog on the scheduled day and said goodbye. Molly ran out to the gate and watched her owner pull out of the driveway. She knew exactly what was going on. I grabbed a leash, hooked it to Molly's collar, and then brought her inside. A couple of other boarding dogs were already there, as well as my own four dogs. I walked Molly to one of the back rooms that had a dog gate in the doorway so she could be safely behind it but still interact with the other dogs if she wanted to.

Then I allowed the other dogs to say hello. Of course, since a newcomer had trespassed onto their territory, they ran thundering toward Molly and made a huge scene. But Molly sat quietly, watching them as if she were thinking, *What a bunch of unruly heathens!*

"Good girl, Molly," I said as I gently petted her head. By then the other dogs had settled down, and Molly went over to the gate to give them a sniff and a shaming look.

Being around so many dogs in so many different situations, I've learned to spot certain personality traits in them. When Molly convinced the other dogs to either walk away or sit quietly, I thought, *Yep, Molly is quite the leader.* Yet she never bared her teeth, growled, or acted in any other aggressive way.

After watching her interact with the other dogs through the gate for several hours, I decided to let Molly out. But I stayed close to make sure everything went okay. Once face-to-face with the other dogs, however, Molly went into pack-leader mode, and within a few seconds she had everyone calm and well-behaved. Then she made herself at home.

Molly stayed with me many times, befriending a little Chihuahua named Tink who was often there at the same time. Molly outweighed Tink by about 35 pounds, but she was her best friend's protector. None of the other dogs could even look at Tink the wrong way with Molly around. She would immediately run to Tink's side and stand beside her as if telling the other dogs to stay clear—*or else*.

Not only was Molly a great protector and pack leader, but she always seemed to be one step ahead of me.

Chasing lizards was one of her favorite things to do outdoors, and in the summertime, hundreds of them lived all around our yard. As soon as Molly got outside, she went into lizard-chasing mode, and she taught all the other dogs to chase them too!

Then she always seemed to know when I thought it was about time to come inside. Not wishing to do so, Molly would round up Tink, and then they would try to hide, hoping I wouldn't find them and interrupt their lizard hunting. Of course, the entire yard was fenced, so I could always find them. Then Molly would give me the most pitiful look, just as if I were the meanest person in the world. So to assuage my guilt, I'd give Molly and Tink a treat...for hiding! *This* was the shameless manipulation of a smart dog!

Giving the dogs that stayed with me free roam of the house helped ease any stress they might feel being away from their owners. Quite often all the dogs would be with me as I worked in my office. Some of them would lie at my feet under my desk, and others would sleep on the dog beds strewn around the room. Molly had a favorite bed; it was huge and pillow-like, and she always made sure no one else got it. Sometimes she even wanted to eat her breakfast and dinner in my office so she could stay near her favorite bed.

One evening, just after I'd fed them, all the other dogs were napping throughout the house. I had decided to feed Molly in my office while I did some computer work so she could be near her beloved bed when she was done. After I put her food bowl down, I sat down at my desk to work.

But then I watched Molly walk over to her bowl, which was

about six feet away from her bed, grab some of the food in her mouth, and take it to her big, poufy bed. She climbed up on it, sat down, and ate the few morsels she'd carried.

I laughed. "You really love that bed, don't you, Molly?" I said as she got up and walked back to her food bowl. She grabbed a few more pieces of food and repeated the whole routine.

Molly entertained me with this scene over and over. I had seen dogs do this before, and it always made me laugh. It's kind of like me taking my food from the kitchen to my bedroom, one bite at a time. As smart as some dogs are, they aren't that good at time management!

But then I saw Molly do something I found hard to believe. She got up from her bed for about the fifteenth time and walked to her plastic food bowl, and then without hesitation, she picked it up in her mouth, took it to her bed, and started eating again. I'm sure I had a look of disbelief on my face.

"Molly, I can't believe you just did that!" I exclaimed as I scooted my desk chair over to her bed. "You are such a smart girl!" Molly gave me a quick glance and then continued to eat her food...from her bowl...on her bed. She had figured out a way to achieve her goal without ever leaving the comfort of her cherished bed.

When she finished the food, she pushed her bowl off the bed with her nose and plopped down for a nap.

> I press toward the goal for the prize of the upward call of
> God in Christ Jesus (Philippians 3:14).

More important than the fact that Molly achieved her goal is the fact that she never gave up. The apostle Paul taught us that importance when he said,

I don't mean to say that I have already achieved these things or that I have already reached perfection. But I press on to possess that perfection for which Christ Jesus first possessed me...I have not achieved it, but I focus on this one thing: Forgetting the past and looking forward to what lies ahead, I press on to reach the end of the race and receive the heavenly prize for which God, through Christ Jesus, is calling us (Philippians 3:12-14 NLT).

Whether the journey is easy or incredibly hard, our goal should be to press on. We press on even when we've been rejected three times, like Molly was, or a thousand times three. We press on when others say we can't. We press on when the enemy throws his snares along our path. We press on even when our past wraps its ugly chains around our feet and tries to hold us captive forever. We press on because God has given us the best reason ever to do so, His Son, Jesus, who calls us out of our darkness and into His marvelous light (1 Peter 2:9).

One amazing day all our "pressing on" will be rewarded. That prize Paul talks about? Well, it's going to be worth far more than escaping any trials or tribulation we encounter along the way. We just have to keep on keeping on. Molly kept on pressing on toward her goal, and she didn't give up. I pray none of us give up either.

I cared for Molly for several years, and she continued to amaze me and remind me how special she was. She always led the pack in her gentle yet purposeful way. And, of course, she always stayed one step ahead of me.

God never does anything by accident, His timing is always perfect, and His plans always line up with that perfect timing. I think of how He set Molly aside, knowing Amy would need her comfort in the days ahead. And even though Molly suffered rejection—not once, not twice, but three times—God knew exactly what He was doing.

God has a plan for each one of us too. And if we keep moving forward, forgetting what lies behind and pressing on toward the goal He's laid before us, *one amazing day* we will grab hold of that perfect plan.

Dear heavenly Father, I can't wait for the day when You reveal to Your faithful ones that prize we seek. In Romans 8:20, Your Word tells us that all of Your creation eagerly awaits that day. I've been blessed to witness Your creation in amazing ways. Thank You for allowing me to see a glimpse of Your glory through that witness. In Jesus's name I pray, amen.

8

THE HEART
OF HOLLIS

Those who wait on the LORD shall renew their
strength; they shall mount up with wings like eagles,
they shall run and not be weary,
they shall walk and not faint.

ISAIAH 40:31

Add four long legs to 80 pounds of pure energy and what do you get? A dog that can clear a four-foot fence—no problem! And that's just what a lovable dog named Hollis did if given the opportunity when I pet-sat for her.

Hollis, 80 pounds of pure love as well, was a mixed-breed dog who'd been adopted from a shelter just in time to save her life. I first met her in November when her owner, Judy, contacted me about pet-sitting while she and her husband took a one-week vacation. I agreed to meet with her to talk about the details.

Judy and Jack lived in a quiet but large neighborhood just a few miles from me. Many of my customers lived in that same neighborhood, and sometimes I visited it several times a day. Now it was early evening as I drove down the familiar main road and turned onto the street leading to their house. It was just across the street from a small but quaint park that had a children's swing set and a little sidewalk that curled around the area. As I pulled into the short driveway, I glanced toward the park and saw some children playing and a young boy walking a Miniature Schnauzer.

A man with dark-gray hair and a medium build stepped from the back door of the house that led into the garage and called to me. "Hello! Christi?"

I stopped and looked his way, and then I backed up a few feet because I was on the walkway to the front door. "Yes!" I said with a chuckle.

"Judy is at the store—still—but come on in and we can talk until she gets here." He stepped aside for me to go through the back door.

I scurried inside and was immediately greeted by a large, short-haired, tan-colored dog.

"That's Hollis, of course, and I'm Jack." He pushed Hollis back with his knee, but Hollis pushed her wet nose into my hand as if to force a pat on the head.

"Hi, Hollis," I said as I stroked her head with both hands, pushing her ears back and massaging behind them. Her tail was wagging so hard that it hit the wall on both sides of the narrow hallway and made a loud thumping sound. I cringed with each thump because they sounded painful!

"Come on in and sit down," Jack said as he led me to the family room. Then he sat in a big, dark blue recliner and added, "Hollis, sit down!" Hollis ignored him and continued to push her nose into my hand. Then she pushed her body against my legs, her wagging tail now hitting me in the thighs. Each wag sent a sharp sting across my legs.

"Hollis, sit down!" Jack said in a much sterner voice. This time she lay down at the foot of his recliner, her tail still swinging back and forth.

Jack explained that they needed someone to feed Hollis morning and evening as well as let her out three times a day. She was just two years old and had a lot of energy (obviously), and she loved to go for walks.

Then I heard someone come in the back door, and Hollis jumped up and ran out.

"Hollis, are you being a good girl?" a female voice said from the hallway. I could hear the rattle of plastic bags, and then a tall woman with short hair came into the room.

"Hello! I'm Judy!" she said as she smiled. She'd entered the room in a larger-than-life kind of way, and I stood and greeted her with a handshake.

"I see you've met our girl," Judy said as Hollis danced around her. We talked for a few minutes, and after she told me Hollis loved to play fetch, she took me to see the fenced-in backyard. It was a medium-sized area with a four-foot wooden fence all around. It was dark outside now, but I could see both next door neighbors' yards. Judy said all Hollis needed was a few minutes of fetch time and then maybe a short walk in the park each day. I wondered, though, how that would be enough exercise for a dog this energetic.

Judy also told me Hollis liked to jump and that on a few occasions she'd jumped over the fence.

"She always comes back sooner or later, though," Judy said as she shot Hollis a disapproving look. I stood quiet, but I wasn't thrilled at that revelation. Then Judy showed me a long lead rope anchored in the ground. She attached it to Hollis's collar whenever she thought she was in the mood to jump the fence, but it was long enough for her to chase a ball.

"I'll probably be using that a lot," I told her. Hollis probably wouldn't feel comfortable with me for a while, and I didn't want to chance her running away. I was afraid she'd get hurt or take off looking for her owners.

I blocked off the dates they'd be away on my schedule and said goodbye when Hollis and Judy walked me to the front door. I would be returning in two weeks.

On that first day, I pulled into the driveway because Judy had given me the garage door code. That way I could enter the house through the door coming off the garage. When I did, Hollis came running, and her boisterous greeting almost knocked me down! But I managed to keep my balance as she backed me up against the door.

"Hi, Hollis! I need to get in so we can go outside," I said. Her wagging tail was once again hitting both sides of the narrow hallway.

"Ouch!" I said, cringing again at the loud thumping.

I pushed my way past the 80 pounds of pure energy and walked toward the door leading to the backyard. "Come on. Let's go outside and play ball!"

Hollis raced ahead of me, wiggling every step of the way. Fortunately, Judy had pulled the end of the long lead that was anchored outside under the back door. That was a great idea, making it possible for me to attach it to Hollis's collar before I opened the door. Otherwise I would have been afraid she'd break my hold on her collar and go barreling outside, possibly jumping over the fence.

"Hold still, girl," I said, trying to attach the lead to a moving target. Finally, I got it hooked and opened the door. She took off like a dog that had spent way too much time being cooped up in the house, so I was thankful to have that lead. As she went charging out, she realized she'd been tethered and stopped just short of the length of yard she could go. She'd probably learned that quickly the first time she was connected to that lead.

I picked up a tennis ball that was lying on a little patio table on the small back porch, and immediately Hollis stood alert with anticipation. I threw the ball, and she jumped about four feet and caught it mid-air.

"Good girl!" I said as she brought it back to me. I threw the ball several more times, and she always caught it mid-air. But by then I was feeling kind of bad because she couldn't really run after the ball. So I decided to see how she'd behave untethered. After all, she was engrossed in the game and probably wouldn't want to jump the fence.

I unhooked her as inconspicuously as I could, hoping she wouldn't even notice she was no longer attached to the lead. I just tried to keep her attention on the now slimy, dirt-laden tennis ball, and when I threw it again, she ran after it, again catching it in mid-air. She brought it to me and dropped it at my feet, and I sighed with relief and threw the ball again.

In one seamless move, she grabbed the ball in mid-air...and flew over the fence!

I'd never seen anything like it.

"Hollis!" I screamed. I ran to the fence, but she was gone. In a breathless state of panic, I ran into the house and out the front door just in time to see Hollis running toward the park across the street.

"Hollis, come here, girl," I called in as calm a voice as I could muster. She never looked back as I watched her run across the park in what seemed like just a few leaps. I sprinted across the street praying no other dogs or cars were around to fuel her freedom spree, but there was no way I could keep up with her. *Lord, please bring her back*, I prayed as I stood in the middle of the park feeling helpless.

Why did I do it? I said to myself. *I never should have taken her off the lead!*

I watched her round the far-right corner of the park, and then she came barreling toward me. "Come on, girl!" I called, praying she would keep coming my way. As she got closer, I stretched out my arms hoping to catch her before she ran right past me. As soon as she got within arms' distance, I grabbed her collar and hung on for dear life.

"Oh, thank You, Lord!" I said with one big exhale. Hollis stood panting, and then she looked up at me with her tongue hanging out. She had made a quick energy run, and now her little escapade was over.

I pulled her by the collar back across the street and to the front door. Once inside, she ran to her water bowl. My hands were still shaking. "We aren't doing *that* again," I said as she drank. Still on wobbly knees, I went to the couch and sat down, and Hollis soon followed. She nudged me with her wet nose, which was dripping with water. Then she laid her head across my lap. *Yeah, she's done this before*, I said to myself. *And she knows how to work it too!*

I couldn't help but stroke her head, and when she placed a big paw on my thigh as if to apologize, of course my heart melted. I spent a few more minutes with her and gave her a treat. However, she must have sensed I was leaving, because she spit the treat onto the kitchen floor and gave me the saddest look.

"I'll be back soon. I promise," I told her as I patted her head. She followed me to the front door and stood pitifully, watching me as I shut the door between us.

My subsequent visits to care for Hollis that week weren't as eventful—thankfully! But it was a challenge to find ways to expend her energy. I took her for walks in the park, but if a squirrel or another dog happened to be anywhere around, it was all I could do to keep hold of her leash. So I started to teach her how to walk on a leash and not bolt after everything that happened to be moving. We made progress, but Hollis was going to need a lot of practice.

Each time I had to leave her, she looked so sad. I was eager for Judy and Jack to return because I could tell Hollis was getting too lonely. Thankfully, the week was soon over, and Hollis's owners returned. Judy told me Hollis was over the top excited when they walked in the door. I always had such a feeling of relief when the pets I cared for were reunited with their owners. It must be so hard on them to be without their family, not knowing if they're ever going to return. If there's anything I wished I could tell them and that they would understand, it was that their family *was* going to return soon, that they hadn't been abandoned.

Judy and Jack became regular customers, and I cared for Hollis many times over a two-year period. On a couple of occasions, I gave her the benefit of the doubt and let her off her lead only to have her once again clear the four-foot fence as if it weren't even there. Thankfully, she went only as far as the front door, and I found her sitting there waiting for me to open it.

I grew to love Hollis so much. She was the sweetest dog and so full of love. I could be having the toughest day, but when I walked in to take care of her, she greeted me as though I was the most important person in the world.

On a cold, dreary December 24 day in 2013, I was scheduled to start caring for Hollis that evening and then through the next ten days until after New Year's Day. That morning I received a phone call from a concerned Judy. Jack woke up that morning not feeling well and his coloring was yellow. She didn't know what to do because they were scheduled to visit their grandchildren for the holidays, and they were both looking forward to it. She asked me what I thought she should do because their doctor's office wasn't open on Christmas Eve.

I knew Jack was jaundiced, and I said she should definitely take him to the ER. She agreed, but Jack was a stubborn man. I had spoken to him only that first evening when I met him and Judy to discuss pet-sitting for Hollis a couple of years earlier. But many times when Judy and I were on the phone scheduling my services, she would comment about something she and Jack had done or something else concerning him in passing. I got to know Jack a little through his wife.

Judy and Jack were opposites. She was open and full of life. Jack was quiet and a man of few words. I understood when Judy told me it would be difficult to convince him to go to the ER—worse yet, on Christmas Eve. But after several hours of prodding, she had persuaded Jack to go. She called and asked me to wait on coming to see Hollis until she let me know what was happening.

Several hours later, she called again. They were still at the hospital, and she asked if I could go check on Hollis.

I pulled into their driveway just a few minutes after speaking to Judy on the phone, and as I got out of my car I noticed how quiet the neighborhood was. I heard no children's voices in the park across the street, and the gray skies combined with the quiet made it seem like such a gloomy Christmas Eve.

I punched in the code for the garage door and went into the house. Hollis came running to greet me. She was so happy to have company. Her wagging tail hit the hall walls so hard this time that it broke the plastic cover on an electrical outlet. "Oh, Hollis!" I exclaimed as I grabbed her tail to see if it had any cuts. But she was unharmed as she crowded me with her wiggling excitement. I pushed her back and picked up the broken pieces of plastic on the floor.

"Come on, girl. Let's go outside," I said as I pushed my way past her. She bounced her way to the back door and waited for me to open it.

I was in no mood to chase a fence-hopping Hollis, so I put the lead on her collar and opened the door. She boisterously ran out into the yard, stopping just short of where the rope would run out. Again, it was so quiet, and I felt as if Hollis and I were the only two beings in the entire neighborhood. I couldn't hear a sound other than the jingling of the metal tags on Hollis's collar.

I threw the tennis ball a couple of times for her, but then I brought her inside. A dismal cloud seemed to have settled over me. I knew Judy was worried about Jack; I could hear it in her voice when she last called. I also knew how important it was for them to see their grandkids at Christmas. I had my own Christmas plans, but I couldn't get excited about them until I heard all was well with Jack.

Once inside, Hollis took off for the back bedroom. I knew exactly what she was doing. That's where Judy kept all of Hollis's toys, and last Christmas I had given Hollis a stuffed orange-and-black tiger with a squeaker inside. It became Hollis's favorite toy, and many times when I came to take care of her, she brought it to me.

I plopped down in Jack's big, blue recliner in the family room, next to the coffee table that sat in front of a couch. Behind that couch was a long table that sat right up against it.

Hollis came running out of the back room with her tiger in her mouth, and in one seamless leap, she jumped over the table, over the couch, and over the coffee table and landed at my feet, where she dropped the tiger!

I sat in disbelief! Thankfully, I hadn't allowed her off the lead because that is exactly what she would have done at the fence. I laughed. I was so thankful for a moment that brightened the melancholy mood that had settled around me like a dense fog.

I picked up the tiger just as my cell phone rang. It was Judy. I could hear the distress in her voice. She told me they were on their way home and that they'd had bad news that meant they weren't going on their trip. Judy said she would call me later and thanked me for checking on Hollis.

My heart was heavy.

Hollis stood in front of me and cocked her head. She had been waiting for me to play tug-of-war with her and her toy. I played with her for a few minutes and then got up to leave. I didn't want to be there when Jack and Judy got home.

Judy called the day after Christmas. Jack had been diagnosed with stage 4 pancreatic cancer.

Those who wait on the LORD shall renew their strength;
they shall mount up with wings like eagles, they shall
run and not be weary, they shall walk and not faint (Isaiah 40:31).

I always viewed my pet-sitting business as a ministry opportunity, and God allowed many incredible situations where I saw Him
work in my life and in the lives of my customers while doing something as simple as caring for people's pets. But as eager as I'd been to
share God's love with my customers, I had to step back and allow
God's timing—not mine—to set the stage for His plans.

Waiting has never come easy for me, but I continue to learn that
waiting on Him is the only way to fulfill His perfect will. My first
instinct is usually to jump on a path and pull God along on *my* journey. But in His perfect and loving patience, He's helped me see that
it needs to be the other way around. I must wait on Him and allow
Him to take the lead as we journey the path together, God always
in front making the path straight (Proverbs 3:6 NIV).

Although I didn't know at the time that the path God was about
to take me down would be difficult, it would be for His own amazing glory. And His timing couldn't have been more perfect.

Over the next couple of months, Judy was adjusting to a life
turned upside down. Jack was having chemotherapy a couple of
times a week, and I was visiting Hollis on those days so she wouldn't
be alone so much.

Judy confided that Jack had become extremely quiet and apa-
thetic. His usual demeanor was rather stern, but he had become

even more detached since his diagnosis. Also, a neighbor who had a friend who was a pastor asked if he could come and pray with Jack. Jack refused the offer more than once before giving in to Judy's prodding. But when the pastor came, he told him to hurry up with his prayer and then ushered him out the door.

God was urging me to make a connection with Jack, and I had begun to ask Him for a way to do that. But based on that incident, I knew Jack wouldn't be open to me sharing anything about God or even mentioning how much God loved him. Each time I visited Hollis while Jack was having chemotherapy, though, I brought the couple dinner. Judy told me how much Jack loved the food. Then a couple of times when he had to be taken to the ER, I visited with him and Judy as they waited for test results. Jack told her later how much he appreciated my being there.

I could feel God chiseling away at Jack's heart, tiny bit by tiny bit.

Almost a year since Jack's initial diagnosis, he became weaker and weaker. Judy said he was sleeping a lot, and he was too thin and continued to lose weight. The doctors told them his tumor was growing.

I knew a great sadness had overtaken Judy's heart because I could feel the heaviness in the atmosphere each time I spent time with Hollis. Hollis could sense things weren't right. She didn't want to play, and she no longer tried to jump the fence. Most of the time I sat in Jack's recliner in quiet stillness with Hollis's head across my lap.

I felt helpless. I wanted to say so much to Jack, but I was afraid of his rejection or that I'd anger him. But now he was weakening, and my opportunities were dwindling. *Lord*, I prayed, *if it's Your will, please give me just one opportunity. Allow me to connect with Jack.*

That same week I had an appointment with a dermatologist because I'd found a small spot on my arm that didn't look right. The doctor decided to do a biopsy, but he said it didn't look like anything to worry about. I left his office and then forgot all about it. It was early December, and the busyness of the impending holidays was starting to take over.

Then I received a phone call from the doctor a few days later. He was shocked to learn that the spot on my arm was melanoma, even though it didn't look anything like it. He wanted me to schedule surgery to have it removed right away. I asked if I could wait until after the first of the year because the holidays were my busiest time of the year.

I'll never forget his answer: "Christi, the longer you leave that spot on your arm, the more the chance that it will take your life. I want you to understand how serious this is. Melanoma is deadly, and it needs to come off *now*. I'm finding a slot for your surgery in my schedule next week."

His words dropped heavily into my heart just as though someone had dropped a load of rocks on top of me. I hung up, stunned, and then I looked at the tiny, pink spot on my forearm that was still healing from the biopsy. I could feel the blood rush from my head, and then a wave of coldness like I'd never felt before washed across me.

I sat down and pulled out my smartphone, and then I researched melanoma. It wasn't good, and I was scared.

I don't remember my exact thought process, but I called Judy. She told me to come over that evening. "Come talk to Jack," she said.

Hollis came running to greet me as I walked into the family room, where Jack was sitting in his recliner. Judy gave me a huge hug. That was so like her. She was so full of love for everyone even though she was going through her own personal hell. Jack was covered with a big, fluffy blanket. His body was so frail. I hadn't seen him in months, and I was shocked by his appearance. He greeted me and asked about my call with the doctor.

At that moment, a huge surge of supernatural strength came over me. As I told Jack and Judy about my conversation with the doctor, God filled my heart with so much grace and love for Jack. Then I shared what God had done for me in my life and how I knew that no matter what happened, I would be spending eternity with the Maker of heaven and earth.

And you know what? Jack listened to every word. He didn't tell me to hurry up. He didn't usher me out the door. He listened. Then he shared what he was feeling. He told me he understood how I felt, that cancer is a horrible diagnosis to receive. I could hear the anger in his voice, but instead of shutting down, he opened up with raw honesty. And when it was time for me to leave, he said I'd helped him, and he hoped he'd helped me as well. I told him he had helped me immensely, and that now I had some small idea of what he'd been feeling.

I wept as I drove home that night. The reality of what God had just done was overwhelming. His timing had been perfect, and I thanked Him for giving me the connection I'd been praying for even if it meant I might be taking the same path as Jack. Somehow, though, it didn't matter. My own diagnosis was worth it because I was able to relate to Jack in a way no one else could at that moment. It was worth it because someday I might see the eternal result of what had taken place in Jack and Judy's family room that very night.

A couple of days later, Jack took a turn for the worse. I wanted to do something, so I wrote him a letter about some of the same things we'd spoken that night in his home. I also wrote out my favorite psalm, Psalm 23:

> The LORD is my shepherd; I shall not want. He makes me to lie down in green pastures; He leads me beside the still waters. He restores my soul; He leads me in the paths of righteousness for His name's sake. Yea, though I walk through the valley of the shadow of death, I will

fear no evil; for You are with me; Your rod and Your staff, they comfort me. You prepare a table before me in the presence of my enemies; You anoint my head with oil; My cup runs over. Surely goodness and mercy shall follow me all the days of my life; and I will dwell in the house of the LORD forever.

I gave the letter to Judy, and she read it to him. Then she called me that same evening. Jack was a man of few words and few things impressed him, but he had made a point of telling her he was touched by my letter. She kept thanking me over and over for writing it.

A few days later, Jack passed away.

I had my surgery the very next day. The doctor was confident they had removed all the melanoma and said that the cancerous cells had not gone deep enough to warrant chemotherapy.

I thanked God for His perfect timing. If I hadn't waited on Him, Jack may not have received what I said to him. But God knew what Jack needed and when he needed it, and He knew what I needed too. Isn't it amazing how He works? How He knits our lives together for His perfect purpose? I believe someday I'll see Jack again—whole and no longer racked with cancer.

Hollis was with Jack when he took his last breath. Her huge heart had been broken, but I knew it would heal. She soon regained her desire to fly over the four-foot fence in her backyard, and neither Judy nor I had the heart to be angry with her about it. Hollis was also a great comfort to Judy as she mourned Jack.

I continued to pet-sit for Hollis for the next two years, and then, sadly, Judy passed away unexpectedly. I had lost a wonderful friend, but Hollis had lost her loving owner. Judy and Jack's grandchildren took Hollis to live with them, and I received several reports that she was doing well and had fallen in love with her new family as deeply as they had fallen in love with her.

❧

Dear Lord, thank You for the times You've reminded me that Your timing is perfect and that waiting on You is the only correct option. Thank You for setting Your perfect plan in motion through a huge-hearted dog named Hollis, which gave me the opportunity to connect to her hard-hearted owner. Someday we'll see the result of our obedience to You, and it will be a joyous day! Please continue to renew my strength as I walk the path You've set before me, knowing You've already prepared it and seasoned it with Your amazing grace. In Jesus's name, amen.

9

FORGIVING TOTO

～～～～

Be kind to one another, tenderhearted, forgiving
one another, even as God in Christ forgave you.

EPHESIANS 4:32

I was excited by what I saw in the local newspaper. I had just started my pet-sitting business the week before, and this was the first ad for my services. But my financial goals were more meager than you might imagine—I just wanted to be around animals all day. Yes, I had four dogs and four horses of my own, but my husband wasn't enthusiastic about having more to feed. Pet-sitting for other people's animals, then, was a way to love more of God's creatures without adopting more into my home. It was a splendid compromise!

One of the calls I received the very next day was from Mary, a long-time resident of the town I had just moved to. She needed to board her two Peekapoos, but she didn't want them in a kennel-type atmosphere. Because both dogs met the weight limit for boarding in my home, we scheduled a time for her to visit my setup and talk about her needs.

It was early January, a cold, dreary, and extremely wet month in my new town. This Florida girl didn't do winter well. I'd grown up where wintry weather lasted about a day, and I certainly wasn't prepared for an actual winter!

As Mary drove through the front gate into my driveway, I was outside shivering and annoyed that all my friends in Florida were enjoying sunshine and perfect weather. She waved through her car window just as a gray-and-white furry face pressed against the window in the backseat. Mary turned off the ignition and opened the door.

"Hi, how are you?" she said in a somewhat distracted voice. Another gray, furry-faced dog had hopped onto Mary's lap from the passenger's seat.

I laughed as I watched her wrap her arms around the dog and put her down on the driveway. Then she got out and opened the backseat door, quickly grabbing a gray-and-white dog just as it was about to spring out of the car.

"Now be nice, girls," she said as she attached leashes to each of their collars. Then turning to me, she said, "This is ToTo," pointing to the shorter of the two dogs. ToTo was all gray with a long fluffy tail. I watched her pull in every direction as far as her leash would allow. Her body stood erect on her short legs as she sneezed and snorted, shaking her head. I also noticed her adorable underbite, which gave her smooshed face even more expression.

"Hi, ToTo," I said, extending my hand toward her. She gave me a blasé look and then pulled the slack out of her leash as she trotted in the other direction.

"And this is Lucy," Mary said, pulling the larger of the two dogs by her leash to bring her closer. Lucy immediately ran to me and stood on her hind legs with both front paws on my legs. "Hi, Lucy!" I said as I petted the top of her head. She wagged her tail and waited for more attention. Lucy had a darker gray, curly coat, white feet and white fur on her chest and face, and long legs and a long, thin body.

"Are they really both Peekapoos?" I asked.

Mary nodded.

"They're very different looking," I said.

"Yes, they're from different places."

We walked around outside as I showed Mary the fenced area where the dogs would be let out to play. I explained that Lucy and ToTo would be around my dogs as well if everyone got along.

But Mary preferred Lucy and ToTo to be kept separate because they weren't much for playing with other dogs. So when I took them all inside, I showed Mary the room Lucy and ToTo could have by themselves. She agreed it was a perfect setup and scheduled a three-day stay for her two girls.

ToTo and Lucy arrived early one morning. Mary had their favorite beds, toys, and treats with her as she brought them to the front door. I could tell she was a little apprehensive about leaving them for the first time, but ToTo and Lucy trotted inside as if they had been there a hundred times before. Mary was nervous, but neither of her dogs seemed to be.

I understood, though. Engaging a pet sitter for the first time is like leaving your children with a babysitter for the first time. I assured her ToTo and Lucy would be well-cared for and that they would receive a *lot* of love. Mary fretfully left her pets in my care.

I had the dogs' suite all set up, and I took the beds Mary brought and put them in their room along with a bowl of fresh water. All the while, ToTo and Lucy were busy running around the house sniffing and exploring. I had put my four dogs in another part of the house, but they knew something was going on and were barking nonstop. That didn't seem to bother ToTo or Lucy, though.

I led the girls into the room where all their familiar belongings were and closed the dog gate across the door so they could see out into the house but stay confined as Mary requested. They went right to their beds and lay down, and soon they were fast asleep. *Good dogs*, I thought as I sighed with relief.

ToTo and Lucy were perfect boarders, quiet and well-behaved. But they were completely different from each other. ToTo didn't like to be held or even touched. Mary hadn't given me much information about how to treat her, but I quickly learned that she was independent, and a couple of times she snapped at me. She didn't make contact, but if I accidentally touched her face or her paws, she wasn't happy.

Lucy was loving and loved to be held, pet, and cuddled. She spent hours on my lap while I worked at the computer. Whenever I sat down anywhere, she was either on my lap or under my feet. And she didn't like it if I gave any attention to ToTo.

When Mary arrived to pick up her dogs, she was relieved that their visit had gone well. She confided that ToTo and Lucy sometimes got into fights. But I assured her they'd been fine while staying with me.

I was glad, but I've been around dogs my entire life, and I've learned to decipher the body language that precedes a brawl or a disagreement between them. Most often, I can stop a scuffle before it happens. My own dogs have learned it's not wise to get into a fight if they see a certain disapproving look on my face.

ToTo and Lucy became regulars, and I loved them like my own dogs. ToTo continued to be somewhat disagreeable and touchy, while Lucy continued to be affectionate and quite agreeable. But I learned to work around ToTo's tendency to be ornery, and I never let her think she had the upper hand (or paw). I wanted her to view me as an authority figure, not someone who was afraid of her. Otherwise, she may have used that in her favor.

One of the things all the dogs staying with me had to accept was getting their paws wiped after being outside. If I didn't do that, I'd be mopping 24 hours a day! All the dogs had to line up at the door and one by one let me wipe off their paws before they could come inside the house. It was amazing how quickly they all learned this routine. Everyone played along...except ToTo. She hated having her feet touched, so I had to pick her up and distract her with a treat. Then while she was busy chewing, I quickly wiped her paws. Thankfully, she never finished her treat before I was finished.

As time went on, I noticed ToTo was becoming more cantankerous, as though she wasn't feeling well most of the time. I mentioned this to Mary, and when she took her in for a checkup, the veterinarian diagnosed ToTo with diabetes.

ToTo needed an insulin injection once a day. I had no problem giving her the injections when she stayed with me; I had given my horses injections many times. And for the most part, ToTo was good about it. But as her health declined, she tried to bite me as I approached her with the syringe.

One morning she was successful. This was no ordinary nip; she clamped down hard on my hand. I had never been bitten like that before, and I retracted my hand quickly and ran to wash it. However, ToTo viewed that action as weakness on my part and subsequently attempted to bite me on other occasions as well.

As much as I loved ToTo, I didn't want her to keep biting me. She didn't give a warning bite each time; she went for blood! I had to tell Mary I couldn't take care of ToTo anymore. Avoiding her difficult disposition was too much work.

It was a hard decision to make, and I hoped I was making the right decision. I had taken care of ToTo and Lucy for more than nine years. They were family, and I considered Mary family.

I called Mary and told her about the one incident when ToTo had bitten me, but I didn't tell her about all the other times ToTo had tried to bite me. She was upset and concerned for my safety. She told me she understood if I couldn't care for ToTo anymore, but she hoped I would. I felt horrible, so I said I would think about it more and get back with her.

Over the next few days, I prayed a lot about my decision. I didn't want to do the wrong thing. I knew it would be difficult for anyone else to care for ToTo, and that broke my heart. I couldn't bear to think of her being with someone she didn't know and who didn't understand her.

To be completely honest, I must admit that my feelings toward ToTo had changed. I didn't trust her, and as much as I loved her, I didn't like her much for biting me. I knew she was just acting on instinct, and I'm sure she wasn't feeling well because of her health issues, but it was hard to overcome my feelings after she'd bitten me.

Be kind to one another, tenderhearted, forgiving one another, even as God in Christ forgave you (Ephesians 4:32).

As I prayed, asking for the right answer, I was reminded about the power of forgiveness. ToTo was a dog whose intentions were without malice but based on instinct. I needed to forgive her if I was ever going to be able to care for her again. That's when God reminded me of my own need for forgiveness.

I've borne the scars of a painful "bite" from others and then carried the poison seeds of unforgiveness—lethal seeds that grow out of control if not destroyed—many times. But when someone has hurt us deeply or caused us pain that we did nothing to warrant, how do we forgive?

The answer lies in one powerful and crucial truth: God, through His Son, Jesus, forgave us.

We don't deserve that forgiveness. We have offended a sinless and perfect God from the day each of us were born (Romans 3:23). It's in our free-will nature, given to us out of love from a Creator who wants His creation to *choose* to love Him, to *choose* to obey Him.

Those who have hurt us sometimes don't deserve our forgiveness either. But God has called us to love and forgive even so. I think forgiving others can be one of the hardest things we ever have to do. It's also one of the most liberating.

I battled the imprisoning chains of unforgiveness for years over a painful event. I would say I had forgiven someone who hurt me, but in reality, I hadn't. Then one day the Lord told me I must forgive this person. *But they don't deserve it, Lord*, I cried in a pool of self-righteousness and pride. Immediately, I heard Him say, *And neither did you, but I forgave you.*

That truth cut to my core.

Sometimes the Lord requires only that we be willing to forgive, and then *He* works out the rest in our hearts. That's how He brought me to fully forgive that person who had caused me incredible pain. Each day I would tell Him I was "willing" to forgive, but I didn't feel the forgiveness in my heart. But then I noticed my spirit felt less and less angry toward that person. Within a month, I was praying for the one who hurt me, something I could never imagine doing before.

One day I realized I no longer felt that pain or anger at all, and I knew I had forgiven that person fully. God had completely changed my heart. The blessings flowed after I obeyed God and forgave, blessings I may have missed out on had I continued to carry that lethal burden.

God doesn't leave us on our own as we try to swim upstream in the raging waters of unforgiveness. If we're willing to allow Him free rein in our lives and our hearts, He can make changes in us we never thought possible. We can forgive those we considered most unforgivable.

As Christians—Christ's ambassadors—we're called to love one another as He has loved us. We are members of His body that best serves a hurting world when we live a life of loving others for Him. And part of loving others is forgiving one another as He has forgiven us.

After praying about ToTo for several days, I decided to continue caring for her. I would just have to find a way to be more careful around her. Mary was relieved by my decision. ToTo came to stay with me many times after that. I found that if I distracted her with a treat while giving her the injection, I could get the medication in and still move my hand out of her biting range before she finished her treat. She never bit me again, and I had forgiven her.

ToTo's health continued to decline as the diabetes led to other health issues. I had been caring for her for almost ten years of her life, but Mary knew it was time to let ToTo go. It was a difficult time for her, but it was also a difficult time for me. It's never easy to say goodbye to any animal I've cared for. ToTo held a huge part of my heart.

A few months later, even though she said she would never do it again, Mary brought home a tiny fur ball. She named her Winnie. Winnie was the cutest puppy I'd ever seen. She was a black-and-white Peekapoo with a tiny black nose and a flat face. She had white fur around her nose that made her appear to have a mustache. A look from her big, round eyes would melt anyone's heart.

One spring day Winnie and Lucy both came to stay with me, and Winnie kept my husband and me on our toes. It had been a long time since a puppy had been in the house, but she kept us laughing the entire time.

I cared for Winnie and Lucy many times after that. Lucy continued to be the lovable dog she had always been. Winnie was a riot, and I grew to love her. I realized that had I not continued to care for ToTo, I would have missed out on the blessing of Winnie.

Dear Lord, thank You for forgiving me even though I don't deserve it. Please help me serve You with a humble heart and a forgiving spirit, especially toward others and even if I think they don't deserve it. Help me, as Your ambassador, see this world through Your eyes and love others as You have loved me. Thank You for teaching me Your truths through Your wondrous creation. In Jesus's name, amen.

10

THE INVISIBLE PET

~~~~~~~~~~

Turn to me and be gracious to me,
for I am lonely and afflicted.

PSALM 25:16 NIV

The fall day was beautiful as I drove down the winding, rural road I lived on. Leaves trickled around my car like giant red and gold snowflakes. Occasionally the wind would capture a few on the way down and make them spiral in reverse, only to let them drift back down again. It was like driving through an autumn wonderland.

I was on my way to meet Mrs. Moore, who had inquired about my caring for her dog in her home. She lived in a neighborhood where I had several customers, so I was sure I'd passed her home many times on my way to other jobs.

When I pulled into the driveway of her yellow, two-story house, the garage door was up halfway, and I could see a blue car parked inside. The lawn was well kept, although only a few shrubs lined the walkway to the door. I grabbed my notebook and pen, and then I got out of the car and walked along the short path to the front door. After ringing the doorbell, I waited quite a while, making me wonder if the bell didn't work or if Mrs. Moore hadn't heard it ring. So I knocked, and almost immediately an older woman answered the door. She was probably in her mid-to-late sixties, and she had chin-length, jet-black hair that seemed to exaggerate her small frame.

"Hello, I'm Christi," I said as I gave her my business card. She smiled sheepishly and took the card as she stepped aside for me to come in.

"Come into the kitchen and sit," she said in her strong, German accent as she led me up a flight of stairs. Her home was modestly furnished yet immaculate. I glanced around, wondering if I'd catch a glimpse of her dog, but I didn't even hear one.

She led me to an oversized table pushed close to the wall in one corner of her small kitchen. Mrs. Moore sat down, leaving me to the heavy, dark chair next to the wall. It could barely be pulled out enough for me to sit down, but I managed to squeeze between the chair and table and wiggle my way onto the seat.

My hostess was quiet as I opened my notebook, ready to jot down any notes.

"Are you looking for pet care while you go away, or do you just need some help on a regular basis?" I asked, hoping to get a conversation going that would give me information. She nodded her head and said she needed someone to take care of her dog while she was away on a three-week trip.

I caught myself looking around once more for Mrs. Moore's pet, but I saw no sign of it.

"Tell me about your dog," I said. Maybe she would go get it— wherever it was.

"She's a Shih Tzu, and she's small," she said, nervously folding her hands on the table in front of her.

I smiled and commented, "Aww, those are very cute and sweet dogs," hoping I could coax some more information from her. But Mrs. Moore just smiled back and nodded.

"When will you be needing someone? Do you have dates yet?" I asked as I turned the page in my planner, ready to write. I was desperately trying to get past our uncomfortable, bogged-down exchange. But she didn't have exact dates just yet. She said she would have to let me know.

I told her my fee, and she said it was fine. Then I closed my planner and wriggled my way out of the seat I had stuffed myself onto minutes earlier. Mrs. Moore got up too, and I thanked her for meeting with me.

"What's your dog's name?" I asked. This was the question that had been sitting in the front crevice of my mind the entire time. I don't know why I was so afraid to ask it. For whatever reason, it seemed like reaching for the forbidden fruit, so I didn't dare take a bite even though the apple was sitting right in front of me.

"Sylvia," she said.

"Well, I'm looking forward to meeting Sylvia."

Mrs. Moore nodded quietly, and then she made her way back down the stairs as I followed behind. I shook her hand and thanked her, and she smiled and thanked me for coming.

"What an odd meeting," I said out loud as I drove down Mrs. Moore's street. But maybe she'd been so quiet because her English wasn't very good.

My mother lived in the same neighborhood as Mrs. Moore, so I decided to visit her on my way home. I told her about my meeting with Mrs. Moore.

"I'm sure I won't be hearing from her again," I said. "Obviously, I'm not someone she wants to leave her dog with. She didn't even want me to meet her, and I didn't even hear Sylvia make a peep. It was all so strange."

"Maybe her dog just wasn't there for some reason."

"Well, I don't know, but it sure was the strangest meeting I've ever had with a potential customer."

That evening I told my husband about my meeting with Mrs.

Moore. "Something seems off," I said. "I can't explain it, but I just have the strangest feeling."

I had forgotten all about my perplexing meeting with Mrs. Moore when I received a phone call from her a couple of days later.

"Hello, this is Mrs. Moore. Would you be able to stop by tomorrow to talk more about caring for my dog?" she asked. I was a little surprised by the phone call, but I told her I could be there at four.

After several pet-sitting stops in her neighborhood, I pulled into Mrs. Moore's driveway right on time. I noticed the garage door was once more halfway open and that the same blue car was inside.

I knocked instead of ringing the doorbell this time, and Mrs. Moore answered immediately.

"Hi, how are you?" I asked.

She smiled and nodded. "Good. And you?"

"Good, thank you," I said as I stepped inside. Once again she led me up the stairs and to the kitchen table, and once again I tried to gracefully navigate the tight space between the table and that chair. I let out a silent sigh and glanced around to see if I might spot Sylvia.

Mrs. Moore sat quietly as if she were waiting for me to start the conversation.

"What other questions can I answer for you?" I asked.

After a moment she said, "I don't have firm dates for my trip yet, but I want to tell you what kind of food I feed the dog."

I waited for her to continue.

"I feed her both canned and dry dog food. I mix it together." Her eyes glanced around the room several times and then back to me.

"Okay, that's fine. Can you write down the exact amounts of each for me? Then when I come I'll have your notes."

"Yes," she said.

I sat quietly for a few more seconds, racking my brain for

something—anything—to say to fill the awkward silence. Then I did it. I took a bite of the forbidden fruit.

"Where is Sylvia now?"

"She's at my son's house."

"Oh, okay." I decided not to question any further. "Is there anything else you would like to tell me or ask me?" I asked as I picked up my planner and wedged it between me and the table.

"No, that's all."

"Okay. Well, why don't you write down exactly how you would like me to feed Sylvia, and then you can leave that on the kitchen counter for me when you go away. But if there's anything else you can think of or need to tell me, just call. Anytime." Then I scooched the chair out as far as I could and held my breath as I wriggled out of my confining position.

"Do you have some idea about when you'll be going away?" I asked once we were at the front door. "I'd like to mark the dates on my schedule so I don't get booked up." I opened my planner, ready to jot down tentative dates.

"Maybe next month?" Her tone was tentative.

"Okay. I'll make a little note, and then if I start to get booked up, I'll let you know."

"All right."

Once more, I thanked her for meeting with me, and then I said I looked forward to hearing from her about the dates for her trip. She smiled and waved as I headed to my car, and I pulled out of her driveway just as perplexed as I'd been after our first meeting. *Something just isn't right*, I thought.

Over the next several days, I couldn't stop thinking about Mrs. Moore and the odd meetings I'd had with her. I drove by her home several times, and each time I noticed her garage door was up halfway and that the same blue car was inside. I concluded Mrs. Moore must live alone. I wondered if she had any family close by. Did her son live in our town? I contemplated checking in on her because I just couldn't shake the feeling there was more—way more—to her story. Something I needed to know.

Have you ever thought of someone you hadn't thought of in a long time, maybe even in years? Or maybe someone crossed your mind out of the blue and you couldn't get that person off your mind but couldn't figure out why? Whenever that happens to me, I consider it an opportunity to pray for the one who's come to mind. And many times, later down the road or even as soon as that very day, I learn that person was in trouble or going through a difficult time and desperately needed prayer. That is the Holy Spirit working.

I started praying for Mrs. Moore. I didn't know exactly what I was praying for, but I asked the Lord to allow me to help her if she needed it.

The next week, I received another call from her. This time she'd left a message on voice mail, once again asking if I could stop by because she wanted to go over a couple more things about caring for her dog. I returned her call and told her I would be there the next day when I was finished with another job in her neighborhood.

On my way to her house, I asked God to help me say and do the right things because I had no idea what the right things to say and do were. And I asked Him for wisdom because by now I suspected Mrs. Moore didn't have a dog, and I didn't know what my purpose was in continuing to meet with her if I was never going to pet-sit her "pet."

A part of me thought this was all a big waste of time. But the Holy Spirit was speaking to me, prodding my heart. I couldn't see a purpose in these meetings, but God had one, and for whatever reason, I had become a part of it.

In her usual quiet demeanor, Mrs. Moore led me to the same spot upstairs—the kitchen table. I had become quite skillful at gracefully sliding into the restricted space offered, and I was already sitting down and facing Mrs. Moore when she sat down.

"Tell me what I can help you with," I said, smiling.

She smiled back. She'd forgotten to tell me that she needed her newspaper brought in every day while she was away.

I told her I could certainly do that for her, but I couldn't hold back my concern any longer.

"Mrs. Moore, do you need anything else? Is everything okay with you?"

"Yes, I'm fine. Everything is fine," she said in her usual timid tone.

"Well, if you need some help with anything at all, please call me. If I can't help you, I'll find someone who can."

She thanked me, and then silence filled the room once more before we made our familiar trek to the front door. But this time she followed me to the driveway. I could tell she wanted to say something, so I turned and waited.

"Thank you very much for coming to see me," she said.

At that moment I could hear the loneliness in her voice and see it in her eyes, allowing me to see her in a completely different way. No longer was she someone who wanted me to care for a pet that didn't exist; she was a lonely woman who needed a friend. I placed my hand on her arm and asked her if she had any family close by.

"I have a son who lives several hours away," she said quietly.

"Does he come to help you with things you need done?" I asked, looking around her neatly manicured lawn.

"Yes, he comes once a month to mow the lawn and helps with little things around the house."

I told her I was glad to hear she had someone she could rely on, and I that I was going to be praying for her.

Her eyes filled with tears as she patted me on the arm and thanked me. It was the most she'd said to me in all our meetings put together. I waved goodbye and then got into my car and backed out of her driveway.

I checked on Mrs. Moore a few times over the next several weeks. I never asked about Sylvia again, and Mrs. Moore seemed happy to have someone to talk to even though she never said much. Still, I could sense she was relieved each time I showed up at her door.

One day when I stopped by, her son was there. I introduced myself and told him I had been visiting his mother on occasion just to make sure she was doing okay. I never mentioned my original intent was to care for his mother's *dog*. We only exchanged small talk, but he sparked my curiosity when he said they would be taking a trip and would be gone for several weeks. He didn't mention when they'd be leaving or needing me to care for a pet or bring in a newspaper. I didn't want to be nosey, so I kept my curiosity to myself. I told Mrs. Moore goodbye and that I would check on her again.

When I pulled into her driveway several days later, her garage door was completely raised and the entire garage had been cleaned out.

A sense of panic rushed through me. I quickly turned off my ignition and went to her front door. I knocked, but no one answered. Then I peered through the side windows of the front door. The small room in front of the stairs was completely empty. All the furniture was gone. I was shocked.

I ran back to my car and pulled my cell phone off the console, and then I dialed Mrs. Moore's phone number. It was disconnected.

I stood in her driveway completely baffled. What had happened? I had no way of knowing, but I remembered Mrs. Moore's son mentioning that trip. But why would they clean out the entire house? It didn't make sense.

Because I didn't know any of Mrs. Moore's neighbors, I didn't feel comfortable going up to their houses to ask if they knew anything. I looked to see if any of them were outside at that moment—then I could ask without knocking on anyone's door. Sadly, I didn't see anyone around.

For weeks I drove by Mrs. Moore's house on my way to other jobs, and I even stopped a few times just to see if someone was there. But the garage remained closed, and the house stood empty.

Turn to me and be gracious to me, for I am lonely and afflicted (Psalm 25:16 NIV).

To this day, I don't know what happened to Mrs. Moore. Perhaps she went to live with her son. Maybe she passed away. But whatever happened, I knew God had orchestrated the whole thing. He'd wanted me to intercede in prayer for her and be her friend for that short period of time. There are no chance meetings or coincidences in our lives when we surrender completely to Him.

When we obey and interact with God's plan, sometimes in blind faith, we never know what the eternal consequences will be. I know what the short-term consequences were in my encounters with Mrs. Moore, though. God saw a lonely woman's need for a friend and He sent His love to her via an imaginary pet named Sylvia.

Our imaginations can never fill the void we have to deeply know our Creator; absolutely nothing on this earth can give us what only

Jesus can. If we dare to let Him, our God *can* and *will* supply *all* our needs (Philippians 4:19).

I almost told God I didn't have time to keep meeting with a potential customer who didn't really have a pet. I'm so glad I listened to the Spirit and allowed God's grace to flow through me to someone in need.

❖

Dear Lord, You are the giver of all good gifts, and You can give us more than our minds could ever conjure up or imagine. We don't need to invent things to fill the void in our lives because You can fill every need we could ever have. But most of all, we need the gift of Your Son. Thank You for teaching me it's always worth my time to be a friend to someone in need. In Your Son's name I pray, amen.

11

THE JOY
OF JOY

Weeping may last through the night,
but joy comes with the morning.

Psalm 30:5 nlt

The front door opened wide seconds after I rang the doorbell. Joy and Steven stood at the entrance to their foyer with smiling faces, a scene that could have been on the front of a Christmas card. Joy had seen the ad for my pet-sitting services in her neighborhood's paper, and because most of my customers lived in that neighborhood, I was quite familiar with it.

"Come in," Joy said. They were a younger couple, and their friendly greeting put me at ease.

"Hi. I'm Christi. It's nice to meet you," I said, handing Joy a business card. When she'd called me, I learned she and Steven would be going away for three days and needed someone to care for her six cats. So I wasn't surprised when a dark-brown-and-tan cat trotted in and curled around my ankles, weaving in and out of the space between them.

"That's Maui," Steven said with a smile.

"He's friendly, but *don't* try to pet him," Joy added.

Before I could ask for clarification, they walked me into the family room. Maui trotted up once more, still weaving around my ankles. A tad nervous about Joy's warning, I resisted the urge to pat him on the head. Instead, I glanced around and noticed several topped-off food and water bowls throughout the family room and the adjoining kitchen.

"The three kittens aren't socialized, so you may never see them," Joy said. "But all you need to do is make sure the food and water bowls are full, and then clean the litter boxes if they need it. The three older cats are a little more socialized, but they still may not let you around them too much."

I laughed a little as I looked down to see Maui still curling around my ankles. *He's definitely social*, I thought.

Joy smiled. "Well, Maui must like you, but everyone mostly stays in our master bedroom and bathroom. That's where we keep the litter boxes."

She motioned for me to follow as she and Steven walked toward the room right off the family room. When I entered the room, I noticed several more water and food bowls, each full to the top. Maui jumped up on the bed, right next to a silver-and-white, long-haired cat who was sleeping in the middle.

"That's Icy," Steven told me. Awakened by Maui's intrusion, Icy stretched across the bed, reaching her paws into the air, and then rolled onto her back. She seemed unruffled by the invasion.

Just then, out of the corner of my eye, I saw a flash of fur dash into the master bathroom. And then I could hear thumping and a scratching sound.

"That's the kittens," Joy said as she walked into the bathroom. I followed. Two panels from the whirlpool tub had been removed so the space underneath was exposed.

"They like to hide under there because they feel safe," Joy said. Then she crouched to look inside the dark opening.

"How old are the kittens?" I asked.

Joy and Steven answered simultaneously. "About twelve."

I stood quiet for a moment as I tried to calculate their answer in my head.

"Twelve weeks? Or do you mean twelve months?" I asked in a half-questioning, half-puzzled reply.

"Twelve years," Joy said. "They aren't *really* kittens. We just call them that. They're Icy's three babies, and we didn't have the heart to give them away."

Joy and Steven both smiled sheepishly, and I laughed. I understood not wanting to give away kittens. When I was growing up, our cat had kittens once, and I wanted to keep every one of them. But my mom had a different plan, so I took them to all my neighborhood friends' houses in a box to find them homes. After all, who can resist a box full of kittens? I came home with my box empty, but I got to see one of those kittens every time I visited the friends who now owned them.

I could still hear thumping sounds coming from underneath the tub, but I never saw the "kittens."

Joy and Steven walked me into the kitchen and showed me where they kept the food and litter. Again, they reiterated that I would probably never see any of the three kittens, and then they told me I'd probably never see their other cat, Arby, who had been a young stray and was also quite shy. Later, I learned that Arby got his name because they found him in an Arby's fast-food restaurant parking lot. Icy, though, was quite friendly, and would enjoy a quick stroke on the head.

Joy and Steven decided to hire me to care for the cats twice a day, and Joy confirmed the dates of their three-day vacation, which started in four days. Then they walked me to the front door, and Maui gave my ankles one last brush before I left.

As I drove through the familiar neighborhood, I thought about my visit with Joy and Steven, who had told me he worked from home and she worked for a large sports network company and often traveled. I was a little taken aback by all the food and water bowls and the fact that there were three, 12-year-old phantom *kittens* I might never see. But their owners seemed nice, and I was happy to take the job.

When I arrived at the house on my first day, I immediately heard more thumping and scampering. Then I caught a glimpse of two furry flashes as they dashed in different directions. I felt disappointed. I'd really wanted to see the elusive kittens, but as soon as the room cleared, a friendly Maui appeared at my ankles. He arched his back as he slid around my legs, and then he flopped on his side right on top of my feet and looked up at me as if to say, *Are you going to pet me or not?*

I remembered Joy's warning. "Darn!" I said aloud. "I forgot to ask her why I'm not supposed to pet Maui." I shot the cat a solacing look and proceeded to the master bedroom.

Icy was on the bed sleeping just like she'd been the day I met her, and Maui scurried in and jumped up to join her. I cleaned each of the four litter boxes lined up next to the shower in the bathroom, but the three food bowls and three huge water bowls were already filled to the top.

With some time to spare, I decided to spend a minute with Icy. She looked like a Persian breed. She was small and had long silver-and-white hair and a flat face with eyes that were always squinted. I gave her a few long strokes as she rolled over, and she seemed to enjoy the attention. Then she yawned and gave me an aloof look.

As I sat on the floor next to the bed and continued to pet her, Maui came to stand close to me on the edge of the bed. Without thinking, I petted his head. He sat for a moment, but then he reached out with his paw, grabbed my hand, and sank his long, incredibly sharp claws deep into my skin. Then he pulled my hand to his mouth and bit down so hard I could feel my skin pop as his teeth punctured the surface.

Instinctually, I pulled my hand to get free, but that just made Maui clamp down deeper to secure his hold on his newly caught prey. I'd never felt pain like that!

I had to do something, but I didn't want to give Maui any more reason to hold tighter. So rather than pulling my hand again or making another sudden movement, I took his paw and unhooked his claws from deep within my flesh. Then I gently grabbed his head and unhooked his teeth before he could get another grip.

As I jumped up from the floor and moved away, I tried not to show much emotion. During my initial visit, Joy mentioned they had security cameras in the bedroom so they could monitor the cats while they were away. I was sure this was all being caught on camera, and that if Joy and Steven were watching, they were thinking, *We told her not to pet Maui!*

I ran to the kitchen sink and poured dish soap all over my throbbing hand. Unfortunately, it stung and added to the deep, piercing pain surging down my fingers. As I washed my hand under the hottest water I could bear, blood flowed from the many puncture wounds Maui's teeth and claws had created just minutes before. It was terrible, and I felt stupid. I certainly understood now why I'd been told not to pet him. But in the moment I had completely forgotten that warning. I just mindlessly and instinctively reached over and petted him. Besides, he'd had that *please pet me now* look all over his sweet, innocent face.

I grabbed some paper towels off the counter and wrapped up my hand, glad I didn't have any more stops to make. I just wanted to get home and doctor my wounds.

I finished checking the food and water in the other rooms and then left, wondering if I would soon get a call from Joy asking about the incident. My hand throbbed all the way home, and as soon as I got there, I poured alcohol all over it and scrubbed it again with soap and hot water.

When I told my husband what happened, he said, "Do you think you should go to the doctor?"

"I don't think so. Just pray!" I said. But I was a little worried.

The next morning my hand was a little sore, but the wounds didn't seem infected. Still, as I left for my morning visit with those cats, I was apprehensive with thoughts of Maui climbing up my leg and attacking me! Thankfully, Joy and Steven hadn't contacted me, saying they'd witnessed the prior day's attack—and *we told you so*.

It was a hot, August day as I pulled out the key Joy had given me and unlocked the front door. I could see the family room from the foyer, and just like the day before, I saw flashes of fur darting in every direction and then out of sight. I sighed. I really had hoped all the cats would warm up to me, but so far only an aloof Icy and a sharp-toothed Maui didn't seem to mind my presence.

The food and water in the bowls in the kitchen and family room area had definitely dwindled since my visit the day before, so first I took care of replenishing the food supply and providing fresh water in those areas. Then I cautiously went into the master bedroom where Maui perched on the bed next to Icy. He watched me for a few moments, and then he went about grooming his paws. I wondered if they still had my blood on them!

As I cleaned litter boxes and topped off more food bowls, he jumped off the bed and again slipped around my ankles. I quietly gasped.

"Please don't bite me," I said as I quivered. Thankfully, he went to one of the food bowls and began to eat. I took a deep breath.

Maui followed me around the rest of the visit, but I wasn't about to fall for his innocent look again.

My subsequent visits were uneventful. I resisted the temptation to pet Maui, and he behaved himself. Icy was often sleeping. The other four cats continued to evade me despite my sitting in the middle of the family room floor and looking as harmless as I could. My hand was better, and there was still no sign of infection. Overall, this had been a successful job.

When Joy and Steven returned home, Joy called to let me know all was well. I decided to tell her about my encounter with Maui because I was certain they'd either seen it on their camera or were going to. She felt terrible. But that was why she'd said not to pet him. He'd bitten her a couple of times as well.

"He looks so innocent, and so you forget and pet him anyway. I've done the exact same thing," she said in a consoling yet distressed voice. She offered to pay for a doctor visit, but I said my hand looked fine. I felt bad that she felt bad, and I wished I hadn't said anything about what happened. After all, maybe they didn't even have a tape of the incident.

A few days later the biggest box of Godiva chocolate I'd ever seen was delivered to my house.

"What on earth?" I said to my husband. "Did you send this?"

He shook his head. He knows better than to send me chocolate, because then he would have to listen to me scold him every time I stepped on the scale for the next month. Inside the shipping box was a card—from Maui. It read, *I'm so sorry I bit you. I hope you'll forgive me.*

I laughed. And my husband enjoyed chocolate for the next month, asking if I thought I could handle being bit by Maui again because it certainly seemed worth it!

I pet-sat for Joy and Steven quite often over the next six years, and during that time Maui and Icy passed away. One of the kittens, Scooby, passed away as well, but I never saw more than a flash of his fur. My own dog, Rocky, also passed away during that time, and I received the nicest card from Joy. That was a difficult period, and I was touched that she took the time to let me know she was thinking of me. She was such a kind person, and, like me, she was a huge animal lover. She'd also given me a key to her home to keep, and I was there enough that the neighbors even waved and made small talk when they saw me.

One warm September day Joy asked if I could help her with Puma, one of Icy's kittens, who was now quite old. She also had kidney problems now, and she needed fluids injected under her skin a couple of times a week. The expense of taking Puma to the vet's office that often would have been huge, but the vet said if Joy could manage the injections herself, she'd save that money. She just needed help because it took two people and four hands.

I agreed to help. I'd given my own animals injections as well as some of my customers' animals, and I felt confident about the task. I also assumed Steven was unwilling to be that extra pair of hands. But when I arrived at her home, Joy told me Steven had taken a temporary job in a different state and would be gone for six months. Otherwise, she said, he would have helped her.

Joy was squeamish about needles, and she certainly wasn't good with inflicting pain on her animals. So she held Puma with her eyes closed while I manned the needle. The fluids were in a large IV bag, and I had to allow about a fourth of the solution to be infused under Puma's skin. Puma was not happy about it, and it took every bit of our combined strength to complete the task.

Sadly, Puma took a turn for the worse a couple of months later and passed away. However, the time I'd spent with Joy while helping her with Puma seemed particularly valuable. I couldn't put my finger on why, but I sensed my help served a purpose even more important than caring for Puma.

Joy's job still required her to travel a lot, and now that her husband was away, she called on me to pet-sit quite often. I was there so much that the remaining two cats—Arby and Necky—no longer ran at the sight of me walking in the front door. Instead, they came running to greet me. Perhaps that was because Joy was gone so much and they were happy to have company, but whatever the reason, I was happy to have won their trust and affection after almost six years. I finally got to see more than just the tail end of flying fur each time I came near, and both cats had won a huge place in my heart.

Necky was almost a carbon copy of Icy. She was silver-and-white and had an adorable smooshed face. Arby was white with gray and black spots. Arby also weighed about 35 pounds! He was huge—and mostly fat! But his delightful personality made his rotund size all the more lovable.

Almost a year after Steven had taken that temporary job out of state, I wondered why he hadn't returned home. Joy also seemed to be struggling. I'd seen nothing specific to make me think so, but my spirit sensed a heaviness whenever I was at her house to care for the cats.

Joy called my cell phone one hot and humid July evening. It was a little odd to be receiving a phone call from her because, for as long as I'd been caring for her cats, she'd always texted me. So after seeing her name on the screen, I answered in a tentative voice.

Joy was frantic. Necky had been stuck under the tub, and she'd had to bash a hole in the wall with a hammer to get her out. She was worried that Necky was stressed over the incident, so she asked if I could come over once a day and check on her. Joy was also working late each evening, and she felt guilty for leaving the cats alone so much.

Joy was grateful when I agreed to come for the next five days.

I walked into Joy's quiet house the next day and instantly felt that same heaviness as a sadness and darkness seemed to surround me. Arby was lying on the couch sleeping. I looked around for Necky and found her sleeping in Joy's closet, where I spoke softly and petted her. She woke up and looked at me, and then she went back to sleep.

I texted Joy and told her all was well. I also took a picture of Necky fast asleep and then one of Arby on the couch before sending them to her. But although the cats seemed at peace, my spirit wasn't. Something wasn't right, and so I prayed.

Lord, I don't know why I feel so uneasy. I'm not sure what's going on, but please help me to discern what it is. If something is troubling Joy, please help her, and please help me to help her.

I gave Arby and Necky one last pat on the head and left. As I drove home, I continued to pray for Joy. And then I heard four words I still think about today: *Draw close to Joy.* I knew who had spoken them, and I remember exactly what I replied without hesitation: *Okay, Lord. I will.* God had a plan, and I wanted to be a part of it. But I had no idea how big and amazing yet painful that plan would be.

Sometimes I eagerly tell God I'm ready to serve Him: *Whatever You want Lord, I'll do!* And I mean every word. But then sometimes I have my own idea about how things should work, inevitably leaving out the hard parts. That must be why the Bible tells us our ways are not His ways (Isaiah 55:8).

When the difficult twists and painful turns of God's plan become part of the deal, my zealousness begins to wane. But as I've grown closer to God, I've realized that without those hard parts, we can't truly become what He created us to be. Without the tears, we will never truly recognize joy.

I asked God how I could draw closer to Joy. She and I communicated through texts most of the time, so I really didn't know much about her. But I knew God would work it all out.

Every summer Joy traveled to an event that took her away anywhere from two to four weeks. Each time I cared for her cats during that period, and she always brought back an amazing gift for me. I was so thankful for her kindness. Now that trip was just a week away, and I was scheduled to take care of Necky and Arby again.

About three days before her scheduled departure, I received a text from Joy asking if I would like to go to lunch with her. I was so surprised, but I knew her invitation was an open door to draw closer to her—an answered prayer. We set a time and place to meet the next day.

At that lunch, Joy told me Steven wasn't coming home; they were estranged. She talked about her past, her marriage, and her feeling of betrayal in many areas of her life, and as we sat in that restaurant booth, she wept. Now I knew why my spirit had felt so sad those last few times I'd entered her home, why I had felt a heaviness when I walked through her door.

I told her God is there in our darkest times, but I could tell she wasn't ready to receive those words. Still, God was working on her heart. He'd asked me to draw close to her, but I knew He would do the rest.

Even though we have the best of intentions, sometimes we Christians can overstep the boundaries God has placed for us and throw a wrench into His plans! I've done that, and then I had to call on Him for damage control. But He is faithful, He knows our hearts, and He knows we're merely made of dust (Psalm 103:14). Even if we sometimes make a mess of His plans, they aren't thwarted by our dusty humanness.

Joy would be leaving for her business trip the next day, and I hoped she would somehow feel God's presence and comfort. I hugged her in the parking lot as we left the restaurant, but I could tell she was hesitant about the physical contact. Only later did I learn she just wasn't a hugger.

Joy's business trip lasted a little over two weeks, and I visited Necky and Arby every day, making sure they had water, food, clean litter, and company. Each time I entered Joy's home, my spirit felt heavy and sad. I prayed for Joy and left a couple of sticky notes on her bathroom mirror with words of encouragement and some Scripture verses, just trying to "draw close" any way I could.

When Joy returned home, she asked me about the sticky notes, and I told her I had wanted to encourage her. She told me that what I'd said at our lunch and those sticky notes had helped her very much, and, amazingly, she asked if she could go to church with my husband and me sometime. I couldn't believe it! I told her of course she could, and I arranged to meet her at our church that very next week.

Joy attended church with my husband and me on many occasions. She always seemed so emotionless, but occasionally I could see that something the pastor said hit home with her. I also laughed each week when he suggested everyone "greet one another with a hug" because Joy would look at me and say, "I hate this part!" But I hugged her anyway every time I got the chance. And I continued to "draw close" every time God opened the door.

A year after Joy started attending church with us, she was about a week away from her big, annual business trip, scheduled to leave on July 1. I had the date marked on my calendar, and I knew she'd text me before she left just to check in.

July 1 came, and I stretched my stiff arms high as I walked into my kitchen around 6:30 a.m. The sun was just coming up, and because its glare hit me right in the eyes through the kitchen window, I squinted as I glanced around to see where I'd plugged in my cell phone to charge the night before. When I spotted it, I picked it up and scrolled through my texts. Nothing from Joy. *How strange.*

Maybe her flight had changed. Or maybe she'd given me the wrong date. That wouldn't be unusual; she'd done that before. But I was sure the dates I had were correct because she'd texted me a few days before and mentioned July 1 was the day. Yet I felt a little concerned, so I texted her: *Joy, today is the day I have scheduled to start caring for the cats. I haven't heard from you, so can you let me know if it is today, or if not, what is the correct day? Thanks!*

As I made coffee, I told my husband I hadn't heard from Joy so I wasn't sure if I was supposed to visit the cats this morning or if it was today at all. He laughed because he, too, knew Joy sometimes got dates wrong.

My phone rang, but since I didn't recognize the number, I didn't answer it. A few seconds later I got a voice mail notification. Joy's neighbor had left a message saying Joy had given my name and number to her as an emergency contact, and that a police officer had come to her door a few minutes ago to say Joy's car had been involved in accident. He was looking for her, and he told the neighbor the person driving the car was probably about 18 years old and didn't have any ID.

I returned the call and asked her which police had come to her door, but she didn't know. I asked her if they told her where the person driving had been taken, but she didn't know that either. All she could tell me was that the officer said the accident happened at 5:00 a.m. and told her on what road it occurred.

I was frantic. I didn't think Joy would let anyone else drive her car, and she had never mentioned an 18-year-old friend. My heart dropped, and my body grew cold.

I started calling highway patrol stations and sheriffs' departments, and finally, I found the right place. The dispatcher said the officer who'd been at the scene wasn't in, but she would get in touch with him and ask him to call me back. Several minutes later, he did.

Anticipating the call, I anxiously picked up the phone. "Hello?"

A deep voice responded on the other end. "Hello, this is Officer Crowley."

"Thank you so much for calling me back. I'm trying to find out who was in the accident you covered this morning. I-I think it was my friend Joy." I tried to speak calmly, but my voice was quivering with concern.

"How old is Joy?"

"She's in her mid-forties, but she looks very young."

"There's no way the driver we life-flighted was in her mid-forties. I would estimate she was more like eighteen years old or so," he said, as if trying to give me some reassurance.

"Joy would never let anyone else drive her car, and she has never mentioned she had a friend around that age," I told him, knowing deep in my gut the driver was most likely Joy.

"The driver wasn't wearing a seat belt, nor did she have identification with her," Officer Crowley said. He also told me no one else was in the car, and no other cars were involved in the accident.

"What was her condition," I asked, even though I dreaded the answer.

"The paramedics worked on getting the young woman free from the car for more than an hour, and then she was life-flighted to the hospital."

I asked which hospital, but he didn't know.

As soon as I hung up I texted Joy: *Joy, where are you? I was just notified your car was in an accident. Please call me! I need to know you're okay!*

I felt sick inside. Deep inside. And in that same deep place, I knew Joy was the driver of that car.

I started calling every hospital in the entire metro area, asking if a woman with Joy's name had come in after an accident. But each time they said no. I was stumped, though in a small way I was relieved. Then I remembered the officer said the victim didn't have any ID on her, so I was looking for a Jane Doe.

I called the same hospitals, and finally someone said yes, a Jane Doe had been brought in early that morning. She immediately connected me to another department, and a calm, kind voice came on the line. The woman asked me my name and what my relationship was to the woman I was looking for. I gave her Joy's name and described her, and then I told her Joy had no family in the area but that I was her emergency contact.

When she asked if I could come to the hospital right away, I asked her if the woman in the accident was okay. But she wouldn't tell me. I explained it would take me about an hour to get there, and as I hung up, tears flowed. I had the sickest feeling in my stomach.

By now my husband was standing near.

"I can't do it!" I screamed. "She's dead. I know it!"

He pulled me close as I buried my head in his shoulder. "You have to," he said in a calm but solemn voice. "She needs you, and you need to be strong."

But I just couldn't. I've always feared seeing horrible things. I don't want to see someone hurt—or worse. I don't know how first responders do what they do. When I was a little girl, my great-grandmother died, and I was brought to the room where her body lay. I ran away as fast as I could. I couldn't bear seeing someone I loved without life.

"Please don't make me do this, God. Not this!" I said aloud.

"They're waiting on you," my husband said as he took my hand and gave it a reassuring squeeze. "You can do this, Christi. God will be with you, and I'll be with you."

Have you ever told God you just couldn't do something He was asking you to do? Or told Him to never ask you to do what you feared because you just knew you wouldn't be able to do it?

The Bible is full of stories about God asking people to do something that either seemed impossible to them or was something they feared. When He told Moses to go to Pharaoh and ask for the release of the Israelites, Moses's response was not an immediate yes. He told God he wasn't the right man for the job because he was afraid to speak in public. And Jonah? Well, he spent time inside the belly of a fish because he didn't want to do what God told him to do.

I can attest that when we do something God has asked us to, even if it seems impossible or we're afraid, He will be right there with us. He'll also equip us with everything we need (Hebrews 13:21) and give us strength we never thought we could muster. Yet we let the enemy convince us that isn't the case. He whispers lies: *You can't do this…God wouldn't ask you to do this…You aren't worthy to do great things for Him…You will surely fail.*

But God's Word tells us a different story, and when we listen to the truth of our God and ignore the lies of the enemy, God can do great and mighty things through us.

Tears still streamed down my face as I threw on some clothes and got into the car. We drove in silence as I imagined having to identify Joy. How would I do it? Why had God *asked* me to do it? It all seemed so surreal. How did I get to this point? I was Joy's pet sitter. I did the fun stuff. How did my role come to this?

The woman on the phone had told me where to go when we arrived at the hospital, and my stomach tightened with every step as we walked toward the Trauma Unit. At one point, I stopped and said to my husband, "Take me home!" But I knew I had to move forward.

We arrived at the unit's front desk, and I prayed under my breath, "Dear God, if this is what You're asking me to do, please help me. Give me strength to do this."

Then I decided to text Joy one last time, just in case: *Joy, I'm so scared. Please let me know you're okay*. I still hoped it wasn't her in that hospital. I still hoped it was all a misunderstanding and that I could go home. I still hoped Joy was on a plane.

A sign gave instructions to pick up the phone on the desk and wait for someone to answer. I did, and when I told the woman who answered who I was, she said to wait at the big, double doors and someone would come for me.

I held my husband's hand tightly, and then the doors opened. A nurse dressed in gray scrubs greeted me.

"Is she alive?" I asked.

"Yes, she is, but she's in a coma. She has severe head trauma, and I want to warn you that she may not look like herself. The accident did a lot of damage."

Then she took my hand and put her arm around me as we walked down a long corridor. Fear surged inside me as I looked around the large room we entered. I could hear beeping sounds and machines hissing as they heaved in and out. A big desk was in the center of the room, and several medical personnel and nurses stood behind it. As I walked with the nurse, my husband on the other side of me, every one of those people turned to watch. They knew why I was there.

I held my breath when we reached our destination. Here, too, machines hissed and beeped. The nurse squeezed my hand as I stood on the right side of the bed and my husband stood on the left. I looked at the person lying there, still praying it wasn't Joy.

The traumatic injuries were just as apparent as the nurse had warned, and I think my brain wanted to shut everything out to spare me the truth. For a moment, I thought, *It's not her.* But then I looked at my husband, and he nodded his head, confirming my excruciating fear.

My knees buckled, and I started crying. The nurse put her arms around me, and when I raised my head, I saw the solemn looks on the faces of everyone around that big desk. "It's her," I said. The nurse asked me if she had immediate family, and I told her about Joy's estranged husband.

"I need to call him," I said.

"Take whatever time you need." Then she gave my hand one last squeeze and left.

Fortunately, Joy had given me Steven's number, and I had it with me. When I reached him, he said he'd take the first flight he could get.

Joy's face was a blur through my tears, but I took her hand.

"Joy, it's me, Christi. I'm here in the hospital with you. You had a bad accident. I know you can hear me. If God's calling you, take His hand. Don't fight what He's saying to you." Then my husband and I prayed. I asked God to give me the right words, and I continued to encourage Joy to listen to His voice.

Necky and Arby were alone, so after a couple of hours, I left the hospital to check on them.

The next couple of days I visited Joy between taking care of her cats. I had contacted Joy's workplace about her accident, and by now others filled the Trauma Unit waiting room. We all took turns sitting with Joy. On Wednesday, three days after the accident, my heart was so heavy. Joy was still in a coma, and the doctors weren't seeing the improvement they wanted.

All day I kept having a vision—every time out of the blue. The best description I can give is that it was like a flash in my mind. Suddenly I'd see Joy smiling, and she was beautiful. I could also see a faint but spectacular background of trees and blue sky.

I wondered what I was seeing and why. That evening I prayed, *God, I just need to know that Joy is okay. I know I'm asking for something You may not give me, but if there's any way, please give me a sign.* I was hoping everything I'd said to her about God and all the times she'd attended church with my husband and me over the last year had touched and prepared her heart for this time. I just needed to know, and I needed to know God was with her.

That very night I dreamed that I received a text from Joy, and in my dream I was angry because I thought someone was playing a cruel joke. The text said, *What??!! I'm perfectly fine!* Then the dream was over.

When I woke up, I was confused. *What kind of dream was that?* But then God revealed the great meaning in that text. I realized the last text I'd sent to Joy was at the hospital when I told her there'd been an accident and that I needed to know she was okay. I had also asked God the night before to give me a sign that she was okay. Since Joy and I had almost always communicated through text, it made perfect sense that God would use a dream about a text to answer my prayer.

Joy was saying "What??!!" because she was surprised that I was asking if she was okay. Then she said she was "perfectly fine"—perfectly, because she was with God. The vision I'd been having the day before was a vision of her in heaven. That was confirmed to me a few days later when the doctors told Steven they thought Joy had died on either Tuesday or Wednesday, that the machines had just been keeping her bodily functions operating.

🐾

Weeping may last through the night, but joy comes with the morning (Psalm 30:5).

My pain over losing Joy was great, but the joy of knowing she was with the Lord was so much greater. Thinking back, I realized why God told me to draw close to her a year before her death. That still amazes me to this day.

God also revealed something else to me. The officer at the scene of Joy's accident told me specifically that he looked everywhere for ID but couldn't find any. But if he'd found Joy's ID, if he'd known more than that the car was hers, he might not have been led to me so I'd be the one to identify her. As hard as that was, I realized how important it was for me to be there to pray for Joy and speak to her.

I believe with all my heart that she heard me tell her to listen to what God was saying to her.

Days later, when Steven went to gather her things from her car, he found her ID in plain view under the front seat.

Steven asked me to speak at Joy's funeral. I'm not one to stand in front of people and talk; I'm much better at getting my point across in writing. But I agreed. I prayed over what I would say, and I asked God to give me the words. I wanted to tell everyone about the vision and dream I'd had, but would people receive that? I was afraid they wouldn't.

I wrote down what I thought God wanted me to say, leaving out the part about the dream and the vision. But I also asked Him to tell me what to do.

Right before the funeral, I explained the dream and vision to the pastor and told him I was afraid to talk about them when I spoke. He said that was an amazing story and encouraged me to share it, but he also said I should do whatever I felt was best. I decided I wouldn't share that part of the story, but then a text came from a friend also encouraging me to share it. I knew God had orchestrated that perfectly, but fear still filled my mind with lies, and I told God I just didn't think I could do it.

When it came time for me to speak, I took a deep breath and walked to the front of the chapel, climbing the four stairs to the wooden podium. My knees were shaking. I had taken my cell phone with me, and I set it on the top of the podium. I looked out into the room filled with more than 200 people, most of them from Joy's workplace, and started reading from my prepared remarks. But I ad-libbed as well. I told them how I met Joy and about the joy of caring for her cats and getting to know her. I told them she had attended church with me the last year and all the things I loved about her.

When I got to the last sentence of what I'd written, I picked up my phone and the paper, but something kept me from going back to my seat. I couldn't move. And then an amazing peace filled me and words began to flow from my mouth. I told about my vision and my dream, and then I picked up my phone and read the last text I sent to Joy before reciting the text in my dream.

When I finished, I looked at the pastor, who gave me a reassuring nod, and then I made my way back to my seat. My husband squeezed my hand and whispered, "You did good." But I knew *who* had spoken those words through me.

When the service was over, my husband and I walked to the foyer and moved against the wall so everyone coming out would have room to get by. But people kept coming up to me, some hugging me and some shaking my hand. They all told me the story of my dream and vision was amazing. I was astonished to learn how many people had been touched by it, both then and in the coming weeks.

I still think of Joy often. I can see her beautiful face in my mind the way I saw it in my vision. It still amazes me how God got me through those painful events I thought I would never have the strength to navigate. But His strength manifests in our weakness, no matter how great it is (2 Corinthians 12:9).

Sadly, Necky passed away soon after Joy's death, and sweet Arby went to live with Steven. Months later I contacted him to see how the cat was doing. Steven told me Arby was great, and that eating was still his favorite thing in the world. He had adjusted well to his new surroundings.

I know I'll see Joy again one day, with all our tears wiped away, and knowing that gives me great joy.

Dear Lord, life is difficult, but I'm so thankful You're there to give me supernatural strength I could never gather on my own. Please remind me that saying yes to You always precedes great blessing even when there's great pain. I long for the day my eyes gaze upon the visible that is birthed from faith, but thank You for revealing Yourself to me in supernatural ways until that day. Help me to release my greatest fears, knowing Your faithfulness and love cover every single one. Through You alone, I can do great and mighty things. In Jesus's name, amen.

12

SAYING
GOODBYE

~~~~~~~~~

To everything there is a season,
a time to every purpose under heaven.

Ecclesiastes 3:1

We've all heard that saying goodbye is never easy. But what if we knew without a doubt that we would see the one we're saying goodbye to again? Wouldn't it be easier then? I'm not suggesting that we wouldn't miss that person but that knowing our goodbye is only temporary would be of great comfort.

If we say goodbye to our spouses in the morning as they head out to work, we often take for granted that we'll see them again that evening. Our goodbye seems routine and without ambiguity. But if we say goodbye to spouses who are heading off to war, our goodbye is much harder and filled with uncertainty. The truth is no goodbye holds any certainty that the separation will be only temporary unless both parties know the One who promises eternal life to those who love Him. Then, and only then, are goodbyes filled with the certainty of reunion.

Have you ever been to a funeral where someone said something like "Heaven just gained another angel" or "He just got his wings"? While those are nice things to say, they aren't filled with the truth of God's Word. Not everyone who dies goes to heaven. The only way we can enter heaven, the dwelling place of God, is by trusting in His Son, Jesus, and admitting we have sinned and fallen short of His glory (John 3:36; Romans 3:23).

If we and our loved ones have trusted in Jesus, admitted to Him that we have sinned against Him and asked for forgiveness, then we can know without a doubt that the goodbyes between us are temporary—no matter what. We will see them again someday, even if death separates us for a period of time.

That truth fills me with peace.

If you don't have that same peace, and you're not sure that when you take your last breath on earth your next breath will be in heaven, you can pray a simple prayer, something like this:

> *Dear Lord, I come to You with a sincere heart. I know I have sinned against You and that I've broken Your heart and done things that have not been what You have deemed righteous. Please forgive me and fill me with Your Spirit so I may live my life anew for You. Make me a new creation in Christ. I believe Your Son died on a cross so that I could live, taking my place and bearing my sins. I believe He rose again and took His rightful place at Your right hand, and that only through His death and resurrection have I now inherited a place in Your eternal kingdom. In Jesus's name I pray, amen.*

If you asked God to forgive you for your sins, God's Word says you are a *new creation* (2 Corinthians 5:17) and that you have been forgiven (1 John 1:9). You are now a child of God, and you have an inheritance in His eternal kingdom (Galatians 4:7; John 1:12). I can assure you that all the inhabitants of heaven are rejoicing at a heavenly party thrown just for you!

During my time as a pet sitter, I had to say a lot of goodbyes to the pets I cared for. Some say when a pet dies, it "crosses the

Rainbow Bridge." But I believe those of us who inherit a place in God's kingdom will have our beloved pets with us there because Scripture speaks of animals being in heaven:

> Your righteousness is like the great mountains; Your judgments are a great deep; O Lord, You preserve man and beast (Psalm 36:6).

> The wolf also shall dwell with the lamb, the leopard shall lie down with the young goat, the calf and the young lion and the fatling together; and a little child shall lead them. The cow and the bear shall graze; their young ones shall lie down together; and the lion shall eat straw like the ox. The nursing child shall play by the cobra's hole, and the weaned child shall put his hand in the viper's den. They shall not hurt nor destroy in all My holy mountain (Isaiah 11:6-9).

> All flesh shall see the salvation of God (Luke 3:6).

> The armies in heaven, clothed in fine linen, white and clean, followed Him on white horses (Revelation 19:14).

> Every creature which is in heaven and on the earth and under the earth and such as are in the sea, and all that are in them, I heard saying: "Blessing and honor and glory and power be to Him who sits on the throne, and to the Lamb, forever and ever!" (Revelation 5:13).

As I've had to say goodbye to the pets I've cared for as well as to my own pets, I've been greatly comforted by reading these Scriptures in God's Word. I know I will see them all again in whatever capacity the Lord has planned and that it will be amazing and wonderful beyond comprehension. First Corinthians 2:9 says, "As it is written: 'Eye has not seen, nor ear heard, nor have entered into the heart of man the things which God has prepared for those who love Him.'"

Billy Graham said, "God will prepare everything for our perfect happiness in heaven, and if it takes my dog being there, I believe he'll be there." I believe that too.

This chapter is dedicated to the pets I've had to say goodbye to. Every single one was special to me, and I miss them to this day. But the Lord not only used each one to teach me something He wanted me to learn; He used each one to bless me in ways I never could have imagined. And one day, one amazing day, I'll see them again. That's my belief.

Dear Lord, You are a God of seasons, and Your Word tells us there's a season for everything under heaven. Some seasons are difficult; some are filled with blessing. But You give us hope that a better season is coming, an eternal season filled with blessings our minds can't even begin to imagine. Until then, give us the grace and strength to live out our seasons here on earth as we wait for Your Son to return, when we'll never again have to say goodbye. In Jesus's name, amen.

IN DEDICATION TO THE FURRY AND FEATHERED ONES I'VE LOVED

Rocky (Rocket Man)—You were the dog love of my life, and what a blessing you were to me. You were sensitive but strong, always leading the pack. You taught me about being strong and allowing God's amazing grace to shine through my weakness. I miss you every day, but I know I'll see you again someday.

Mick—You were a strong and beautiful horse, and I loved your beautiful, black mane. You were a great companion and protector of your herd. I loved your gentle spirit, and no matter how much the others picked on you, you were always willing to forgive. You taught me that gentleness is a greater virtue than being tough.

Benson—You were one of the smartest dogs I've ever known. My husband and I used to joke that when you stayed at our house, we had to be careful not to say anything incriminating in front of you because you went home and repeated everything you'd heard to your owners! You were a joy to care for, and I loved you so much. I'll never forget the day I heard it was time to tell you goodbye. You taught me to never take anything for granted and how important it is to be thankful every day.

Benny (Benny and the Jets)—Besides being Benson's best friend, you were such a sweetheart, and I loved having you come stay with me. Everyone loved you. You got along with all the other dogs, and you were a great peacemaker. You also taught me about the importance of loving others, even those who sometimes make loving them difficult.

Happy—You were exactly like your name and one of the sweetest dogs I've ever met. Even though you were only here for a short while, you brought so much happiness to those who were blessed to spend time with you.

Ripley—You were so beautiful, and one of the most regal Australian shepherds I've ever seen. I'll never forget all the fun we had playing fetch. You had such a gentle soul, and you loved your sister so much. You left us way too soon.

Scotty—You were the most special boy, and you brought your owner so much happiness. You were also a champion lizard chaser, a trait so well-mastered by a West Highland terrier. I don't understand why your life was cut so short, but I do know so much good came from it. God exchanged beauty for ashes. We'll see you again someday—I'm sure of it.

Norton (Norty)—You were such a good dog. You kept my dog, Bella, on her toes, and you gave her some fierce competition when playing fetch. I always had your favorite bed ready for you when you came to stay, and you were so gracious. God always has a plan, and while I don't understand why you were taken so soon, I know all things work together for good for those who place their trust in the Lord. I'll be seeing you again.

Sophie—You were the apple of your owner's eye. I only knew you a short time, but I quickly realized why you were so loved. You were the best watchdog, and you are so missed.

Lexas—You were a princess, but you were so sweet. Like most Shih Tzus, you had a mind of your own, and you let everyone know it. I'm so thankful I had the blessing of caring for you for more than three years of your seventeen here on earth.

Icy, Puma, Necky, Scooby, and *Maui*—I miss you "kittens" all so much. You had the most amazing role to play in the most amazing of God's plans. Thank you so much for being the vehicle God used to do great and mighty things!

Rolle—What a heart of gold you had. Even when you weren't feeling well, you always tried to make things easier on me. You were one of the biggest dogs I've ever cared for, but you were such a special boy. You are greatly missed.

Roxie—Like most West Highland Terriers, you had such a zest for living. You loved hiding from me when you thought I was cutting your lizard-chasing time short, and you kept me laughing each time you came to stay at my house. You always had time for a hug. You will always be missed.

Carl—I'll never forget meeting you for the first time. I was intimidated by your huge size and regal appearance, but you taught me never to judge based on looks because you turned out to be the sweetest, gentlest dog I'd ever known. Besides being so smart, you were loyal and a great protector. I'll never forget your gentle soul.

Shelby—You were such a good example for your little sister, Hollis. You were a well-mannered and calm dog, and a joy to care for. It broke my heart that I never got the chance to say "So long." I have a feeling I'll be seeing you again, sweet girl.

Rocko—You certainly stayed true to yourself! I won't forget the lesson you taught me—ever.

Jazzy—I loved your snort and your short, little Boston terrier legs that came running whenever I opened the treat jar. You were the chipmunk-chasing champion of the universe! You also gave the best kisses ever. You taught me that happiness is enjoyed most when shared.

Frazier—You were the perfect guest and the perfect gentleman.

Nothing ever got your feathers ruffled. I could always count on you to go with the flow. Your favorite place was in my bed and under the covers. Even though you were a Miniature Pinscher, there was nothing small about your heart.

Dizzy—The first time I met you, I didn't think you would ever accept me because you were so shy. But from the first time you came to stay with us, you proved me wrong. You became my shadow and were never far from my lap. You kept everyone in line even though you, as a tiny Chihuahua, were smaller than all of them. I was blessed to care for you for almost ten years.

To To—You always kept me on my toes, but you were such a good dog. It's hard to believe we spent so many years together. I will always love you, and I still think of you often.

Shiloh—You had the biggest, most trusting heart I've ever seen in a horse. You taught me to never give up, not even when things looked hopeless.

Gideon—A dog who will always have my heart. I will never, ever forget you. See you later, sweet boy.

The destination remains the same.
The change lies within the journey.
In faith, hope, and love,

Christi

ABOUT THE AUTHOR

Christi Grace left the corporate world to work each day in the company of animals. As a professional pet sitter, Christi spent 12 years sharing God's love with the animals she cared for, and, of course, with their owners. Her human-interest stories have appeared in various publications. Christi lives in Georgia with her three horses, four dogs, and one devoted husband.

You can connect with her on
Instagram @thefurrysideoffaith.

READY TO RIDE?

From her many years in the saddle, horsewoman Rebecca Ondov offers this inspiring collection of horse stories that will touch your heart with wonder. Saddle up and ride with her to discover the unique personalities and extraordinary devotion horses reveal and the amazing ways they change lives. You'll meet…

- Blackie, a spirited horse who helps turn a young man's life around
- Tuk, a frisky colt who becomes a long-awaited answer to prayer
- Gus, a gray gelding who provides comfort and hope
- Sedona, a castaway horse who proves redemption is always possible
- Starlet, a filly who inspires a girl to get involved and make a difference

Rebecca, author of *Horse Tales from Heaven*, has gathered the best horse stories from her life and the lives of friends to inspire you and provide a window into God's amazing love and provision.

Inspirational Stories from
Life in the Saddle

HEAVENLY
Horse
STORIES

REBECCA E. ONDOV

DISCOVER GOD'S WISDOM ON THE TRAIL

Horses, like all of God's creation, are a reflection of His nature and His immeasurable love for you. Horsewoman Rebecca Ondov is excited to share with you the spiritual lessons she learned during her 15 years in the saddle, guiding pack trips and as a professional wilderness ranger.

Each chapter opens with an inspiring Scripture verse, tells a thrilling story of life on the trail, and ends with a heartfelt prayer. As you read these heartwarming tales, you'll learn more about

- facing your fears
- receiving God's forgiveness and forgiving yourself
- embracing your struggles
- following His direction when it differs from yours

Heavenly Horse Stories will delight you, teach you, and draw you closer to God. Saddle up to hit the trail in search of wisdom!

OVER 100,000 COPIES SOLD

Four Paws *from* Heaven

Devotions for Dog Lovers

M.R. Wells ❧ Kris Young
Connie Fleishauer

LIFE IS BETTER WITH A DOG

With more than 100,000 copies sold, *Four Paws from Heaven* is a surefire hit! Now with a fun new cover, three talented writers and dog masters share wisdom gleaned while walking through life alongside four paws. Through dog tales and human stories, this pack of short, enjoyable devotions focuses on spiritual lessons, including:

- who we are on the inside matters
- rebellion blocks blessings
- boundaries are for our own good
- using our talents glorifies God
- if we always bark, we won't hear instructions

Pet lovers will find encouragement and guidance for their own life through invitations to reflect on the love, companionship, and insight dogs give to those who love them.

To learn more about Harvest House books and
to read sample chapters, visit our website:

www.harvesthousepublishers.com

HARVEST HOUSE PUBLISHERS
EUGENE, OREGON